Love Letters

from an

Extraordinary Marriage

REMEMBER HOW

I Love You

➤➤   ◄◄

Jerry Orbach
and Elaine Orbach

with Ken Bloom
foreword by Sam Waterston

A Touchstone Book
Published by Simon & Schuster
New York   London   Toronto   Sydney

Touchstone
A Division of Simon & Schuster, Inc.
1230 Avenue of the Americas
New York, NY 10020

First Touchstone hardcover edition November 2009

TOUCHSTONE and colophon are registered trademarks
of Simon & Schuster, Inc.

Photo credits are on page 190.

For information about special discounts for bulk purchases, please contact Simon
& Schuster Special Sales at 1-866-506-1949 or business@simonandschuster.com.

The Simon & Schuster Speakers Bureau can bring authors to your live event. For
more information or to book an event contact the Simon & Schuster Speakers
Bureau at 1-866-248-3049 or visit our website at www.simonspeakers.com.

Designed by Joy O'Meara

Manufactured in the United States of America

10   9   8   7   6   5   4   3   2   1

Library of Congress Cataloging-in-Publication Data
Orbach, Elaine.
Remember how I love you: love letters from an extraordinary marriage/Jerry Or-
bach and Elaine Orbach with Ken Bloom; foreword by Sam Waterston.
    p. cm.
    1. Orbach, Elaine. 2. Orbach, Jerry. 3. Actors—
United States—Biography. 4. Dancers—United States—
Biography. I. Bloom, Ken. II. Title.
PN2287.O63O73 2009
792.02'80922—dc22
[B] 2009012590

ISBN 978-1-4391-4988-1
ISBN 978-1-4391-6011-4 (ebook)

Contents

Foreword

by SAM WATERSTON

JERRY ORBACH WAS A MAN I knew for his talent and accomplishments before I ever met him. We were contemporaries, and even before *Law & Order* our paths rarely crossed professionally, I had him "in my sights" all along. He could do things I couldn't, like sing and dance, remember jokes, and tell them. There was plenty to envy and lots to admire: the extraordinary skills, the "touch" that made audiences love him, and the first-class work he was always doing, usually for very long runs in big successes, usually on Broadway.

Meeting Jerry, though, he saw to it that envy was impossible. He was too engaging to envy—too much fun, too easy to be with, too even keeled and level headed. And he gave you to understand that, even if he was awesome, he didn't want you to be awestruck. He wanted you to join the club, take it easy, share a laugh, take a look at things as they are, and not get too excited about yourself, anything else, or him. The more I knew Jerry, the more my admiration for him grew.

Friendship came easily to him, so easily that you almost didn't notice, as if things had always been that way, and why ever would they not? With him leading, in the same natural way, my wife, Lynn, and I came to know and be friends with Jerry and his wife, Elaine—to discover her way with laughter, her courage to look things in the eye, that gathered energy of hers that dancers can come with. And we got to see the clear-eyed optimism and hope they brought to everything, including especially his long fight with cancer.

And, through all that, we came to know a little about the love that they shared.

It was at Jerry's memorial, when some of the poems he had written to Elaine were read, that I found out Jerry was a poet. And, whether he wanted admiration or not, it was that fact that led me to an admiration I have never gotten over. Okay, he knew how to shoot pool better than I did, how to hit the high notes, and get airborne, and stay on the beat. But reading the poems reveals something extra. They're elegant miniatures from a tall poet. As you'd expect, coming from him, they're clever, they sound like him, they have nice felicities of expression, and they're full of wit, charm, and grace. They also reveal—so easily that you might not even see it happening—the size of his heart and the amount of love for Elaine there was in it.

Enjoy.

—*Sam Waterston, 2009*

Introduction

"Hiya, kid."

Those little words changed my life forever. They were the first ones Jerry Orbach ever said to me, backstage during a rehearsal for *Chicago*. It was the beginning of a twenty-five-year love story filled with adventure and laughter and fun. It ended too soon—but will always be a part of me.

One of the many delights of Jerry, a side of him that perhaps his fans didn't see, was his sense of romance. It was that, coupled with his brilliant wit, that led him to write me a little poem nearly every day, before he went off to work on *Law & Order*. The poems were a lot like the man who wrote them—fresh and simple, deviously witty, and deeply loving.

Over the years, without my realizing it, the poems piled up. I would read and enjoy each one, then toss it into the big soup tureen given to us by producer David Merrick, which still sits in my kitchen—until one day, I noticed that the top of the tureen was popping off! The little poems, scribbled on the backs of pages from a page-a-day cat calendar, were overflowing their container. They had become a kind of history of Jerry's and my wonderful life together—the work, the friends, the family, and the fun, but mainly the love story we were in the process of creating each day.

It never dawned on me to gather these poems in a volume while Jerry was alive and writing them. Over time they were simply a part of our daily lives. I saved them because I couldn't just crumple them up and throw them away. I felt that they were my special poems, for my eyes only, and I never dreamed I'd be sharing them with the world. But at Jerry's memorial service, our friend Jane Alexander read a few of the poems to friends and strangers for the first time. I wanted to give people another insight to what their beloved friend was like in real life, because in the movies or on the television screen Jerry's true persona didn't come out.

After the service it was suggested that I gather some of the poems into a book. So, I reread them, reliving the feelings of when I first found them on my breakfast table. Because they were written almost daily, reading them today reminds me of the life we had together. Jerry was always giving me strength and happiness through the poems.

But before I get to the poems, I hope you'll excuse me for first telling you a bit more about my husband and best friend.

Of course, you probably know him as Detective Lennie Briscoe on *Law & Order*. His character was a no-nonsense, tough but fair cop always ready with a quip. For twelve seasons he starred on that show—and he can still be seen nearly every day in reruns—but he was equally successful in films and the theater.

Here are some roles you might remember: Jerry appeared with Treat Williams in *Prince of the City*, in Woody Allen's *Crimes and Misdemeanors*, and, perhaps most memorably, for those of a certain generation, in *Dirty Dancing*. Our friend Richard Brown tells a story about that one.

Jerry and I took a trip to Greece with Richard and his wife, Zora. We were sitting in a taverna on a little Greek island when a smiling older man came over to us and said something to Jerry that we didn't understand. Nobody on the island spoke English, so we had the man write it down. As soon as we got to the island of Santorini, Richard found someone who spoke English to translate the words on the paper. He read it and looked up quizzically. "I don't know what it means," he said, "but it says, 'We love you *Dirty Dancing* Daddy.'" Jerry laughed. "It's Jake! He follows me all over the world."

Lovers of the Broadway theater know him from his many stage appearances. Jerry gave more performances as a leading actor in Broadway musicals than any other actor ever! He got his start off Broadway, in the legendary production of *The Three-penny Opera* and in the original cast of the longest-running show in American theater history, *The Fantasticks*. He soon graduated to starring roles on Broadway in *Carnival! Promises, Promises, 6 Rms Riv Vu, Chicago,* and *42nd Street*. And it was his role in *Chicago* that would prove a turning point in both our lives.

When we met, I was the standby for Velma Kelly, Chita Rivera's character. (I'd taken the job rather grudgingly—never dreaming that my destiny was at stake.) After a career on Broadway (beginning at age nineteen) and in national tours, that was my last stage role—by choice. After that, I'd take on the part of Mrs. Jerry Orbach—to me, the plum role of all time. While I was in the wings watching Chita and absorbing Velma Kelly, I guess I was absorbing Jerry Orbach, too, and vice versa. Three years later we were married. On the evening of our twenty-fifth anniversary, he wrote me a poem, the last lines of which were, "We made it to the silver / let's go for the gold!" Unfortunately, that was not to be.

Jerry's life was never about fame, celebrity, or wealth. Rather, he chose to focus on compassion and kindness. Jerry was a regular guy—a working actor—never your typical star. He didn't have a publicist, no entourage, and he seldom took limos, preferring the subway. We never had a staff and we never bought an apartment—we always rented. We never had a summer house or a country getaway—but we had lots of love and laughter, and those were our priorities.

Jerry at his writing desk, the soup tureen full of poems to Elaine at his side

At first Jerry started writing the poems at 2 a.m. after coming home fresh from his poker games. He wasn't able to kiss me good night, and he'd be asleep when I'd wake up, so he wrote me a good-morning poem. But I suppose the poems really got going because of Jerry's punishingly early shooting schedule on *Law & Order*. In order to be on the set on time, he often got up before 5:30 a.m. He always gave himself forty-five minutes to shower, shave, make the coffee, have some yogurt, read the morning paper—and write me a poem, which he left next to my coffee cup. Oh, those little slips of paper started my days with such love and smiles! Now, looking over them, I feel as if I'm seeing a diary of our lives together.

These poems and this book keep our relationship alive for me in a special way. Not a day goes by that I don't think about Jerry. I'm not pining for him, or wishing that he were here, or mad that he left me. The sadness and grief you feel gets put in the back of your heart. I know he's still with me, and these poems tell me *why* he's still with me. I believe he's very happy that they're nurturing me again. Out of the hundreds and hundreds of silly, smart, moving, beautiful poems Jerry wrote, I've selected some I thought you'd enjoy. Some are about the weather, about what time he planned to be home, about what he read in the paper, or what he was shooting that day—but they were all about love. They're my love letters.

In this fast-paced, plugged-in world, the simple act of putting pen to paper and writing a note to someone you love is a surprisingly bold and romantic gesture. What's more, it's *permanent*—you can hold a love note in your hands, take it out, and read it over and over again. My love poems from Jerry are keepsakes that I will treasure forever. My wish is that this book will give you a glimpse into a loving relationship that was always growing and everlasting. But even more than that, I hope it inspires you to sit down and write something—a poem, a letter, even just a single line—as a memento to someone you care about.

I hope Jerry's words bring you a little of the joy they have given me. I hope they help you appreciate the love you have and value every day with family, friends, and partners. And if you were a fan of my husband, I hope they bring him alive for you just a little bit, as they do for me whenever I reread them. Enjoy.

As Jerry always said, "Onward and sideways."

—*Elaine Orbach*

Jerry's Early Years

→→   ←←

*J*EROME (JERRY) BERNARD ORBACH was born in
the Bronx in 1935, and although his family moved
around a lot in the years that followed, he told me that he always considered himself a New Yorker. Jerry's father worked for
the Neisner Brothers chain stores, managing their restaurant
counter services, though as a young man he'd had some experience working in vaudeville. His mother had reportedly sung on
the radio, though Jerry didn't remember this himself. I guess
you could say show business was in his blood.

The family moved constantly throughout Jerry's early life.
His father's job led them to a number of towns, including
Wilkes-Barre, Pennsylvania; Plymouth, Massachusetts; Springfield, Massachusetts; and back to Wilkes-Barre before settling
down for his high school years in Waukegan, Illinois.

Perpetually being the new kid in the town was difficult, and
Jerry found that humor was the way to ingratiate himself with
the other kids. Since he had skipped two grades in elementary

school, Jerry was always the youngest kid in his class, but even so, he hit his adult height early, so he was always a head above most of his classmates. In high school, he was on the swimming team and hung out with the "tough kids." Jerry told me that his humor caused him to be well liked by his fellow classmates, and his size and association with the JDs (juvenile delinquents) protected him from any hassles. He loved to sing and was encouraged by his teachers to keep up his love of performing. In a way, Jerry's high school experiences remind me of the characters he was to play in his career—tough guys with sensitivity.

Jerry and Rita Gardner in The Fantasticks

Jerry graduated high school in 1952, at the age of sixteen, and worked in summer stock theater in Wheeling, Illinois. He enrolled in the University of Illinois, and in his sophomore year he transferred to Northwestern University. But he was restless for the "big time" and thought that if things were going to happen in his acting career, they were going to happen in New York. Jerry left Northwestern at the end of his junior year to try to conquer the Big Apple.

When he arrived, he joined the renowned Actors Studio and went right into the legendary revival of Kurt Weill and Bertolt Brecht's *The Threepenny Opera* starring Lotte Lenya. Jerry was in good company, with soon-to-be-renowned actors like Ed Asner, Bea Arthur, John Astin, and Jerry Stiller all beginning their careers in the show. After three years in *The Threepenny Opera*, Jerry was offered the lead role of El Gallo in the off-Broadway musical *The Fantasticks* in 1960. Jerry introduced the classic song "Try to Remember" in that show, and the play itself went on to be a massive success, running for forty-two years and becoming off-Broadway's longest-running musical. But the show's beginnings were a bit more modest: Jerry remembered the cost-cutting measures on that first run, where the producers had just a $900 budget for the set and about $500 for costumes. He swore he even wore some of his own clothes on the set to save money!

Jerry's film appearance actually preceded his stage career, though he didn't make much of a mark in films. In the late 1950s and early 1960s, he acted in such films as *Mad Dog Coll; Ensign Pulver,* and *John Goldfarb, Please Come Home.* None of his roles was particularly important, but they gave Jerry a taste for film acting and the occasional boost in his income—he only received $45 a week for acting in *The Fantasticks,* and by then he was a young husband supporting a wife and two children.

Jerry left *The Fantasticks* to make his Broadway debut in producer David Merrick's *Promises, Promises,* a musical based on the Billy Wilder film, *The Apartment.* It was to be a career-changing part. Jerry won the Tony Award for the role of Chuck Baxter, and the play (with music by Burt Bachrach) ran for more than three years. (You might remember a classic Bachrach song from the play called "I'll Never Fall in Love Again," which hit the Top 40 charts.) This success, so long in coming, opened a lot of other doors for Jerry in the theater world. He costarred in two notable revivals, *Guys and Dolls,* for which he was nominated for a Tony Award, and *Annie Get Your Gun,* costarring Ethel Merman, who returned to the title twenty years after originating the title character. He went on to star in the musical *Carnival!* as well as a number of plays, including Bruce J. Friedman's *Scuba Duba* and *6 Rms Riv Vu,* in which he met his great friend, producer Ed Sherin, and Jane Alexander.

I had seen Jerry in *Promises, Promises* and *6 Rms Riv Vu* as well as *Carnival!*—I was a big fan of his work. Then came *Chicago* with Jerry Orbach, Gwen Verdon, Chita Rivera . . . and me.

Jerry wows 'em in Promises, Promises

Elaine's Beginnings

➤➤ ◄◄

I WAS BORN IN PITTSFIELD, Massachusetts, the middle of three children. My father was a barber. He passed away when I was very young, leaving my mother destitute. That's when I became the first papergirl in Pittsfield.

My brother and I split a big route. He got the bike and I got the bag. From the ages of ten to sixteen, I walked that route with the heavy bag. I made my rounds after school—leaving little time to socialize with my friends. It was ballet classes, paper route, dinner, homework, and bed. I was on scholarship at the dance department of the Community Music School of Pittsfield. Just like Jerry, I had a teacher who believed in my talent. She took me to New York and the School of the American Ballet. I auditioned for George Balanchine and was accepted into the school under a full scholarship. And that's how I got to New York at age seventeen.

I was at the top of the dance hierarchy in Pittsfield, but I soon realized I was a little fish in the big pond of New York. The first summer I was in New York, I was placed in the professional ballet class with Jacques d'Amboise and Melissa Hayden and budding ballerinas like Patricia McBride. They were my pals, but I just knew it wasn't for me. Coming from an Italian family, I couldn't starve myself—the ballerinas only ate apples and yogurt—and I knew I didn't want to be fourth swan on the left.

One day I went downtown to the Winter Garden Theatre and saw *West Side Story*. Sitting in the darkened theater, I thought, "Oh my God, they're dancing in heels and they don't have their hair in a bun. I gotta do this. It's more fun." I was told I needed to get my Equity card if I was going to dance on Broadway. So I auditioned and went to summer stock in North Tonawanda and did a season of musical comedy in the chorus. I was bitten. I was having a wonderful time, plus I was getting paid for it. Over the next few years, every time I auditioned I got the job. I continued to work in summer stock, and with each job I got better and better roles. Then I came back to New York and auditioned for my first musical, *Fiorello!*, and I got the job. I was nineteen years old and in my first Broadway musical.

Elaine Cancilla in Promises, Promises

Next I was cast in *How to Succeed in Business Without Really Trying*. Bob Fosse was brought into the show during rehearsals to help with the choreography. He liked me and kept pushing me down front, closer to the audience. I also became a favorite of *How to Succeed*'s composer and lyricist, Frank Loesser. I had the kind of voice that went up to the balcony without miking. Frank loved loud voices and would fondly say to me, "Hey, Guinea lady, sing it alone." Not only did I meet Bob Fosse, with whom I was to work on several shows, but I also had my first glimpses of Jerry. During *How to Succeed*, some of my fellow dancers and I discovered a secret passageway between the 46th Street Theatre and the Imperial Theatre, where Jerry starred with Anna Maria Alberghetti in the musical *Carnival!* On our breaks, when we weren't needed on stage, we'd sneak over to the Imperial and watch Jerry and the rest of the cast. Little did I know that I would eventually marry Jerry.

More Broadway shows followed, including Meredith Willson's *Here's Love*; Kander and Ebb's first musical, *Flora The Red Menace*; *Baker Street*; and *Sweet Charity*. During the latter show, an agent signed me and said to me, "No more chorus jobs for you." I was in the national tour of *Sweet Charity*, playing one of the leads. Then my career turned to summer stock. For eight years, I was a featured lead in such theaters as the famous

Melody Top theater in Milwaukee. I starred in many shows including *South Pacific* and *The Unsinkable Molly Brown*.

Then I got the call from Bob Fosse to join the company of *Chicago* on Broadway. I didn't realize I was meant to be there. Fate had a reason and that reason was to meet Jerry. Though I was in lots of Broadway shows at the same time Jerry was performing in musicals, our lives were parallel tracks that never crossed—I had never met him. We were even performing on the same street sometimes but didn't know each other. Who knew that my destiny was to be his wife?

Jerry never forgot his roots when he was growing up in Waukegan during his high school years.

AUGUST 1998

Before the great bird spans the sky
my labors will be through.
then back uptown I'll quickly fly
by three or maybe two!
We'll eat some dinner
watch TV, and have a lot of fun,
because you are the world to me
Love, the Waukegan son!

Jerry attended Northwestern University outside Chicago and attended the Actors Studio in Manhattan. Instead of "frigging" he used to say "farging."

> *I studied operatically*
> *in Shakespeare I was trained*
> *just like Professor Higgins,*
> *I said "In Spain it rained."*
> *So now I'll go encounter*
> *the farging "Unexplained."*

Even when we had been married for years, to Jerry I would always be his "Broadway dancer." Jerry always loved to dance, and whenever we went out he would never tire of dancing with me—and I was surely grateful for that, as I never tired of dancing with him, either.

APRIL 2000

Last night we tried to jitterbug
but now I have the answer.
I'll just watch while you cut a rug,
my super Broadway dancer!

How We Met

*I*T WAS 1975, I was back in New York, and Bob Fosse wanted me to stand by for the part of Velma Kelly in the original production of *Chicago*. (When the original actress is sick or on vacation, the standby assumes the part.) I didn't want to accept the job, since I was a star in summer stock theaters throughout the country—I wanted to return to Broadway in a leading role. But my agent convinced me to take the part, because the show was shaping up to be a Big Deal on Broadway. Now, of course, I realize that I was destined to join the show because it was during the run of *Chicago* that I was to meet Jerry.

Standbys don't have dressing rooms, so I was always hanging out offstage in the wings. The first couple of weeks I stood behind the curtain, watching the show and studying the lead actress's choreography so I'd know enough to step in at a moment's notice. And of course, from my vantage point I couldn't help but notice Jerry, who was playing the lead role of Billy Flynn. When Jerry made his entrance, he would pass me and off-handedly say, "Hi, how you doing?" After I learned the role, my presence offstage wasn't as crucial, so I found myself wandering around a bit. I remember Jerry saying to me, "Look, if you don't want to stand in the wings, you can use my dressing room. When I'm not on stage, I'm playing poker with the crew." So, when my feet hurt from standing around, I'd go sit in his dressing room. It was a lucky break . . . except for the fact that he really *was* out playing poker with the crew, so I rarely had a chance to really talk with him. But as the weeks went by, we started to find opportunities to chat and had fun just being flirty. I began to perk up when he came by. While I was in the wings absorbing Velma Kelly, I guess I was absorbing Jerry Orbach also.

I had bought a rabbit fur jacket that winter, and whenever Jerry saw me he'd always say, "Here comes the wabbit." And somehow the nickname stuck. The flirting continued, and one day, my closest friend from way back, Alice Evans, came to see the show. Afterward, we went to Joe Allen's, the leading theater restaurant and bar. It was packed to the rafters with the post-theater crowd, with no place to sit at the tables or the bar. Jerry called us over and said we should stand with him and some other guys from *Chicago*. By the end of that evening I was

Jerry with M. O'Haughey and Gwen Verdon in Chicago

sitting on his lap. He told me he wasn't giving up his seat; his legs were tired from the show. But I was welcome to share it with him! Jerry took me home in his car and we necked a little bit. I said good night, and as I went inside, something inside me was already saying, "Whoa!! What's this?"

But Jerry had a lot on his plate, too—he was fresh out of a divorce and had two young boys. Because he was just out of his marriage there were no traditional "dates." He spent the weekends with his kids. Our dates were just going out after the show when we had the chance or slipping out for dinners be-

Jerry and Elaine in Chicago

tween shows on matinee days, sometimes with one of his kids joining us. I even paid for my own meals at the beginning. It was a committed relationship to some degree—we liked each other a lot—but it was very low key.

We were together in the show for eight months. By that time we had really become a well-established couple and were not seeing anyone else. When the show closed, the national company was ready to go out on tour, but I wasn't a part of it. We were both unhappy, but we both had to work. Jerry left town with the *Chicago* production, and I took an in-between job with a show in New York. The first stop on his tour was Boston. After just a few days, Jerry came back down to New York on his day off and asked me to join him on the tour—he missed me too much, he said. It didn't take me too long to pack my bag. I called my agent and told him I'd be taking a break; needless to say he thought I was crazy. I thought it was a bit nuts myself, but I knew I had to see where this thing with Jerry was going. I toured with him for the next several months.

When the tour was over and we found ourselves back in New York and, of course, Jerry had to get a job. After all, he had alimony and child support. He was offered the National Tour of Neil Simon's *Chapter Two,* and I was asked to be a standby in the production. One day, after rehearsals for the play, Jerry came home to my apartment. He took this little box out of his jacket and got on one knee, saying, "I have to do this right." I asked what was in the box and Jerry quoted a line from *Chapter Two*, "It's a car." When he gave me that engagement ring, it was a complete surprise to me. I was really going to be married!

We ended up in Los Angeles when the tour ended, and after a few days in the sun and surf we decided to stay there. Jerry thought he might try movie and television work. As we were biding our time, we decided, "Let's get married." Things were a little easier and more spontaneous then, somehow. So we invited the cast of *Chapter Two* and some of our relatives who lived on the coast. Jerry's costar, Herb Edelman, was his best man, and one of my oldest and dearest friends from *Sweet Charity*, Kathryn Doby, was my maid of honor. We had our reception at Ed Asner's house; Ed was still very good friends with Jerry from back when they costarred in *The Threepenny Opera*. It was my dream come true.

Jerry didn't always write me a poem. When he was out of town working on a show and I was back in New York City, he wrote me this note:

Jerry and I on our wedding day

August 24, 1987

Hi Wabbit!

Look who's writing a letter! And at 6 o'clock in the morning yet!

The dawn is beautiful hitting the mountains, and one bird got up as early as I did, and he's yelling his beak off for everybody else to wake up too.

There's dew on all the cars and nobody around but a

newspaper delivery truck and a security guard driving by once in a while.

Because of this crazy schedule I don't often have time to think, but when I do, I think of you. I know that saying "I Love You" is an everyday thing, almost a habit, like "good morning" or "good night," but I do love you very much, and I miss you even more. I can't wait to see your face and kiss it! Then I'll work my way down. . . . Oh, never mind, that way lies madness! Anyway, it's time for Lights, Camera & Sit Around! I hope by the time you get this your back is all better, and I'll talk to you tonight. You are the best thing that ever happened to me, and wherever you go today, shopping, massage, voice lesson, etc., know that you're on my mind and in my heart.

I Love You
Jer XXX's

Jerry never forgot the details of our relationship and used our history in the poems.

OCTOBER 1997

When did I fall in love with you?
When I asked you to Boston?
What matters how our love began,
(I sound just like Jane Austen!)
I only know I love you still,
and I'm not being clever,
I always have and always will
our love will last forever!

XXXX's
Jer

Two Bananas

*J*ERRY KNEW POKER. HE'D say, "It's the only game where you're in total control. If you don't have the cards, you can just put the hand down."

Before Jerry's success on *Law & Order* really solidified his career, Jerry was in between jobs a lot. He went over to his club, the Lone Star Boat Club, and played poker to make what we called our "unemployment money." Jerry never filed for real unemployment, so a few times a week he was in there with the big boys.

The Lone Star Boat Club has a long history. Back in 1887, two young Jewish men from Texas (who happened to be on a sculling team) wanted to relocate to New York City and to join a health club. All of the major clubs in New York were restricted, so, in 1887, these guys opened their own club, which they named the Lone Star Boat Club. It was primarily Jewish but not exclusively. The club moved around through the years before settling in its current location on West Fifty-fourth Street.

After Jerry and I were married we moved to Fifty-third Street, and the minute he stepped foot inside the Lone Star, it was love at first sight. There was a workout room with an Olympic-size swimming pool, a sauna, and a party room where wives could come—the only room where women were allowed. Otherwise it was all bellies, cigars, and men in towels.

The Lone Star wasn't your typical yuppie health club, no Mylar and mirrors and plants. The card table was always filled with poker, hearts, and pinochle players. Even though the men were all older than Jerry, there was a fabulous camaraderie. Later on he said that not only was I a golf widow, I was a Lone Star Boat Club widow. He was a member there for almost twenty-five years.

Those were his out-of-the-show-business friends. We went to some nice weddings and bar mitzvahs, as well as funerals, with the members of that gym. They were a part of our life. Every Saturday and Sunday from 11 a.m. to closing and on Wednesday evenings Jerry was there playing poker and exercising. After he got the part on *Law & Order*, he was still a regular there, saying, "I have to keep my legs strong to jump on a criminal."

On the poker table there was a fruit bowl. No matter if he won or lost, Jerry always tried to bring home two bananas from the Lone Star for us to have in the morning. He knew I like a banana with my cereal or grapefruit. Even when he'd lose, which was rare because he was very good at poker, he nearly always left with two bananas. He felt he saved the night with those two bananas.

He'd come home at 2 a.m. and I was already be asleep, and when I woke up the next morning he was still asleep. Since he couldn't kiss me good night or kiss me good morning, he wrote me a poem. These were the first poems he left me. When I came into the kitchen, on the table I found a poem and two bananas.

He either wrote about how much he lost or how much he won . . . plus two bananas! One time, Jerry found a lot less money in his pocket at the end of the evening and, to add insult to injury, there were no bananas. Even when he came out in the red, he made it fun and optimistic, but in truth we had some tough times when the cards didn't go right.

The very first poems were written late at night, after Jerry returned from his poker games at the Lone Star Boat Club and was too wound up to go to sleep.

FEBRUARY 1999

These silly little poems I write,
each couplet and quatrain,
are not just exercises
calisthenics for the brain.
They're meant to say I love you,
and in fact: (no big surprise)
to make sure in the morning
I'm the first thing in your eyes!

XXXX's
Jer

→≻   ≺←

Holy mackerel
sweet Rosy O'Grady
I won two bananas
and 1580!

Har! Har!
Jerry

➤➤   ◄◄

Wait till you
read what follers
you'll give out whoops
and hollers
you'll go buy shirts
and collars
I won a thousand dollars!!

XXX's
Jer

➤➤   ◄◄

My luck has turned so bad,
I don't know what to do!
I lost 175
and there's no bananas for you!

XXX's
Jer

⤗ ⤛

I played tight
I played thrifty
I won 2 bananas
but lost 250.
The hell with this
I'm going back to work!

XXX's
Jer

Salad Days

✈   ✈

*A*FTER WE GOT MARRIED, Jerry decided that he'd give Hollywood a try. Although he was a star on Broadway, it seems his reputation didn't travel to the West Coast. Though he had appeared in such hits as *The Fantasticks; Carnival!; Promises, Promises* (for which he won a Tony Award!); and *Chicago*, the casting folk in Hollywood didn't seem to know who he was. Jerry was always amazed at the way Hollywood operated, and at the huge gulf that loomed between Broadway and Tinseltown. Jerry told me about one particularly humbling meeting with a clueless Hollywood casting director. Résumé in hand, Jerry sat down with the director, who obviously had no idea who he was. After giving the résumé a cursory glance, the man looked up at Jerry quizzically: "Oh, you were in a carnival?" obviously expecting him to be an accomplished fire-eater or sword-swallower. Jerry had to explain that *Carnival!* was actually an award-winning musical (and had been Jerry's Broadway debut in 1961). The casting director looked at him blankly. Jerry didn't get the gig.

Just when we were at our lowest point in L.A., we were saved. From out of the blue, acclaimed director Sidney Lumet called and asked if Jerry would come back to New York to star in a movie he was filming out there, called *Prince of the City*. You never saw two people pack so quickly.

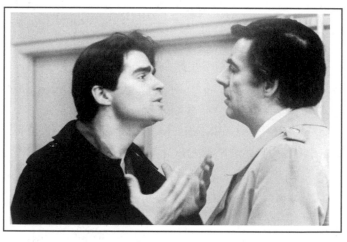

Jerry and Treat Williams in Prince of the City

Jerry's acting in *Prince of the City* (a drama about NYPD police corruption, in which Jerry played a hard-boiled cop . . . go figure) got noticed by critics and the public, and the film was nominated for several Academy Awards. He costarred with a young Treat Williams, who became a friend. Jerry's portrayal of a conflicted New York City cop brought him a lot of notice. With this success under his belt, Jerry revived the idea of a film career. But people still weren't knocking on his door. The only work he had was voiceovers for commercials.

Just then producer David Merrick and director Gower Champion called him and offered him the lead in the musical *42nd Street*, which he happily signed on to. It was a great decision— the play was a huge hit on Broadway, and the lead role of theater director Julian Marsh was a perfect fit for Jerry. He was back doing what he loved (theater) where he loved to do it (New York).

Jerry in 42nd Street *with Karen Ziemba*

Jerry was with the show for five years, an eternity in the theater, but it was a great and very stable time for us.

But Jerry eventually got the itch to move on. So, for the second time, Jerry made the rounds, trying to start a film career. From around 1985 to 1993, he acted in some wonderful movies, including *F/X, Crimes and Misdemeanors, Last Exit to Brooklyn*, and even the iconic movie *Dirty Dancing*. But there were many lean days, and we were sometimes just barely getting by.

Jerry used to refer to these early "lean days" later in life, when he finally had a stable and lucrative gig on *Law & Order*.

> *The night is dark*
> *the land is cold*
> *but somewhere out there*
> *is TV gold.*
> *I'll dig it up*
> *refine and blend it,*
> *then bring it home*
> *so's we can spend it!*
>
> *The day is bright and sunny*
> *I've broken out in sweat!*
> *But I can't see my bunny*

because she's not up yet!
So I will go to work now
and try to be breadwinner
the next thing that I hope to say
is "Honey, what's for dinner?"

One of the roles that has come to personify Jerry is his portrayal of Jake Houseman, the father in *Dirty Dancing*. When he began filming *Dirty Dancing* in September of 1986, we just thought it was going to be a nice little movie set in the woods. I went to visit him on long weekends, and believe me, the accommodations were rustic. Jerry was staying in one of those homes with a common living room and television. In his room he had a bed, a chair, a sink, and a pull-chain lightbulb hanging from the ceiling.

Since the budget was low on *Dirty Dancing* (a mere $5 million), nobody in the cast was getting paid very much money, so Jerry negotiated a "point" (or 1 percent) of the gross. Little did we know that it was going to be the monster hit that it would become. That nice little movie was great for us financially, and Jerry became known as "Baby's father" for the rest of his life.

The movie's success finally opened up a lot of doors for Jerry in the TV and movie worlds. After *Dirty Dancing*, Jerry was given a chance to have his own series. A couple of years earlier, Jerry had been hired by producer Peter Fischer to appear in a few episodes of *Murder, She Wrote*, the mystery series starring Angela Lansbury. Now Peter offered Jerry his own television series, *The Law & Harry McGraw*, a spin-off of the character he played on *Murder, She Wrote*. Unfortunately, it wasn't the hit we had been hoping for, and its cancellation after just one season was a big disappointment to both of us. But it led, albeit indirectly, to another opportunity . . . Jerry's defining role as Detective Lennie Briscoe on *Law & Order*.

Jerry and the lovely Kelly Bishop in Dirty Dancing, *a movie that would follow him around the world*

Peter Fischer was a big fan of Jerry, both on-screen and off, and their friendship continued for the next two decades.

Some twenty years ago, in Murder, She Wrote's *first season, we were looking for someone to play a somewhat seedy Sam Spade clone . . . and as fate would have it, Jerry Orbach was looking for some television work that would introduce him to a wide audience that New York theater couldn't provide. Thus did Broadway's most talented song-and-can't-dance man become TV's Harry McGraw, slightly larcenous, slightly inept, but with a heart of gold and a streak of loyalty a mile wide.*

Jerry appeared as Harry three or four times on Murder, She Wrote, *and it was such a pleasant experience I noodled with the idea of a spin-off. This requires a huge leap of faith on the part of any producer, because a self-titled series gives you no wiggle room to deep-six the prima donna if he becomes impossible to work with. I'd been lucky with Angela Lansbury and Peter Falk (on* Columbo, *another series I worked on) but some other experiences had been agonizing in the extreme. But I was sure Jerry was the real deal and we plunged ahead. Without much resistance the network agreed to a thirteen-episode commitment and we were on our way. I thought.*

One of the first phone calls I received post-deal was from the programming chief, and it went like this. "We have to get together and talk about replacing Jerry Orbach." This self-styled network genius with a room temperature IQ told me emphatically that Jerry was not, and never would be, a television star. (Say, boys and girls, can you spell Law & Order?*)*

Well, nobody got replaced and we assembled a happy cast and embarked on a really terrific experience. I discovered early on that, like me, Jerry was a lover of word games, trivia, and other mind-bending pursuits, so naturally, I ditched my usual obligations and visited the set to match wits with the master. Most of the time I ended up being the grasshopper.

It was about a month into shooting when Jerry came to me with a respectfully couched request. (How unlike a TV "star.") In our next episode there was a part for a perky waitress at Harry's favorite watering hole, and since she was married to a second-story man about whom the plot revolved, this was no two-line walk-on. Jerry wondered if perhaps . . . ahem . . . we might consider casting his . . . ahem . . . wife. Wife????? I screamed to myself inwardly without so much as quivering a lip. I hesitated only momentarily. "Can she act?" I asked. "Absolutely," Jerry replied. Well, the straightest of straight arrows had just guaranteed her performance. How could I say no?

Jerry as Harry McGraw

Within days Elaine arrived ready to go and instantly won our hearts. Not only could she act, she was gorgeous, funny, and looked great in her skimpy waitress outfit. If the show had lasted longer we would have made her a regular. But alas, 'twas not to be. Done in by a mediocre time slot and network indifference, The Law & Harry McGraw *foundered on the shoals of cancellation. We fought hard to keep on going. We failed.*

Some time later, I received a call from Dick Wolf. He wanted to know what my working experience had been like with Jerry. Most of us knew Dick had been saddled with a couple of egotists previously, and I guessed he was gun-shy. I told him that working with Jerry would be the happiest relationship he could ever hope for. Somehow I suspect he already knew that. Have you ever met anyone who had an unkind word to say about Jerry Orbach? I haven't, and I doubt I ever will.

The roles continued to come—*Beauty and the Beast* and *Crimes and Misdemeanors* were big—but mostly there were only voice-overs and some episodic television. While Jerry was at the poker game winning what he called his "unemployment money," I was at home watching *Law & Order.* I remember saying to Jerry, "Honey, you have to watch this, it's really good."

One day Jerry got an offer to guest-star as a lawyer on the show. He was very good, and I guess he did such a good job that when Paul Sorvino was having trouble with his asthma because of the cold winters in New York, Jerry was put on the short list to replace him. Jerry joined the series in the middle of its second season.

At Jerry's memorial service, Dick Wolf reminisced about Jerry's joining Law & Order.

After I asked Jerry to take the role he responded, "Look, I'm kinda interested in this, but I don't know what you're looking for in this character. There's really not much on the page. There's not a lot of character development in anything you do." I had a tendency immediately to agree with him because it's kinda true. He followed up by asking me, "So, what do you want?"

"You know, Prince of the City *would be just fine."*

He looked at me for a couple of seconds and said, "Got it." That was it. It was the only acting note I gave to Jerry in thirteen years.

When he walked out of the fog in his first episode and was castigated by Mike Logan, played by Chris Noth, for not answering a page, he responded, "For what I was doing I don't wear a beeper." It encapsulated a sense of charac-

ter—world weariness and fun that never left through three partners, twelve years on the mother ship (as we called the original Law & Order*), and the beginning of* Trial by Jury. *He was not only the ultimate trouper, he was also the ultimate team player, a guy who never let anybody on stage with him down and was so generous with new partners, new actors, and people making their first appearance on the show. He was the dad to a lot of people over the years. His incredible generosity of spirit is what I continue to think about every time I think of him. And in a business in which schadenfreude is a polite emotion, Jerry is the only person in show business who I never heard a negative word about either as an actor or as a person. I honestly believe that his theatrical, film, and television legacy is not only unimpeachable but will go on for years and years. But his ultimate legacy is being a true gentleman in the sense of being a gentle man.*

"Shirley the waitress" was an inside joke with us. It's a reference to a character I played on Jerry's first series, *The Law & Harry McGraw*. We lived in an apartment building, in number 20A.

→>   <←

From Velma Kelly to Molly Brown
from Shirley the waitress to Chapter Two
there aren't ten people in this town
who really know what you can do!
But my love grows in every way
so screw 'em all but 20A

Xxxx's
Jer

Jerry as Detective Lennie Briscoe on the set of Law & Order *with (from left) Jill Hennessy, Chris Noth, and S. Epatha Merkerson*

Law & Order

Law & Order CHANGED everything for Jerry and me. The show finally brought us the long-hoped-for stability he had been working for his entire career. Jerry loved the cast and the crew, and they loved him right back in return.

The winters were the hardest part of filming the show for Jerry. He'd have to get up at dawn, because in the script it always seems that the corpse is found early in the morning or after midnight, and they're often discovered in an open space like Central Park or Riverside Drive. But that was the job and he loved it.

→⊱ ⊰←

SEPTEMBER 1998

The night is dark, the land is still
the dawn has not yet broken,
no warbling of a whip-poor-will
no traffic in Hoboken.
But Law & Order *pays the bill*
and so I have awoken!

XXXX's
Jer

→⊱ ⊰←

SEPTEMBER 1998

I'm off to Brooklyn (How insane!)
since winter is upon us.
But I'll come back, thru snow or rain,
if I swim the Gowanus!
When I leave before dawn

the day stretches on—
I wish I could kiss you—
I already miss you—
I don't even have time to yawn!

XXXXXXX
Jer

→→   ←←

NOVEMBER 1999

Darkness still upon the land
can't see the Jersey border,
who's up you say?
One hearty band—
The folks from Law & Order*!*

XXXX's
Jer

→→ ←←

To Brooklyn I must go today
to shoot some Law & Order.
And then I'll sing a song at BAM,
Then back across the border,
then down to Windows on the World?
This day is some tall order!

→→ ←←

FEBRUARY 2000

The bad news is I worked till one,
and now it is one thirty.
The good news is I wasn't digging ditches,
     getting dirty.
The best news is tomorrow
I can sleep like Rip Van Winkle,
unless, much to my sorrow,
I get out of bed to tinkle!

→→   ←←

MARCH 2000

This early morning rising
becomes a way of life.
I'm marching off to work again
(without a drum or fife).
On yogurt and some berries
cut by my lovely wife.
Now, Isn't this too cutesy
for a former "Mack the Knife"?

One of the strengths of *Law & Order* was that it didn't rely on any one character to carry the show. And because it was such a tight-knit ensemble, the cast quickly became good friends. Sam Waterston and Jerry came from the same mold, the same era, and the same theater background. They were a funny team because Jerry would have liked to have been hired more as a "legitimate" dramatic actor, while Sam always wanted to sing and dance. They were both stars in different arenas, they were both smart as tacks, and they became good friends.

Sam could never tell a joke. One day, Jerry said, "I have a joke that you can remember. A horse walks into a bar and the bartender looks at him and asks, 'Why the long face?'" That became Sam's joke.

Sam recalled Jerry's positive attitude on the set, as well as his lack of patience. "Jerry always declared, 'I love everything about this job, including what I don't like about it.' There was deceptive simplicity in his improvised humor, too, which was also good humor.

"One example: Jerry's sitting by the monitor waiting for camera rehearsals with the second team to end so that the actors could be called to the set. There are a few things wrong and quite a few adjustments to be made. And they keep rehearsing one thing and another and another. Jerry liked work all right, but he especially liked getting work *done*. This time he just said in his deadpan way, 'How much rehearsal does the second team need?' Simple. Funny. Jerry-like jokes. Laughter never made anything worse and Jerry liked making things better."

One reason Jerry was so prepared was that he had a photographic memory. First, he'd read the entire script through to get a sense of the first part of the show. He'd learn the lines while they were blocking and getting the camera moves. After they blocked the scenes several times, they sent the actors away and spent an hour or two setting the lighting. The only times there were glitches were when day players came in and wanted to be so perfect so badly that they'd mess themselves up. On days like that, when it was take thirty-two or so, Jerry put an arm around their shoulders and walked them around and told them in the most fatherly way possible, "They're not going to take you to jail if you don't say this right. You know the part. Just say it." Really, Jerry was thinking, "I gotta get home, kid, let's just do this one now." And as soon as they got confidence, which often came from Jerry because the director was busy with the cameras and lighting, it went okay.

Jerry on the set of Law & Order

The show gave us a sense of being able to breathe easier. It was a job to him, but he loved it. He loved when they were on hiatus and he loved going back to work as if he were going to the first day of school. He'd say, "I couldn't sleep. I got up before the alarm. I feel like a kid with a new pencil box."

Because Jerry wrote these poems while having breakfast before being picked up to go to work, *Law & Order* was often the subject of the poems.

MARCH 1997

Today I've a pickup at 7:45
in less than a hiccup
I'm at Riverside Drive!
Then Zabar's for coffee
and back down to here
on West 52nd, the QE2 Pier!
In case you find all these locations confusing,
just think how much worse
if we really were boozing!

XXXX's
Jer

→> <←

APRIL 1997

The sun has not yet risen,
the land is still and dark.
Guys who should be in prison
are roaming Central Park.
Who else is up, construction guys?
The ones who drive the tractors?
Some firemen, cops and garbage men,
And . . . Oh, yes! Movie actors!

XXXX's
Jer

⤜ ⤛

JANUARY 2000

A chilly Thursday morning,
the wind could freeze your liver!
And so, where are we filming?
113th and the River!

XXXX's
Jer

A lot of Jerry's poems about working on *Law & Order* were about rushing home to me after filming. Jerry told his driver that as long as he never touched the brakes, they'd never get hit from behind. He really wanted to get home to me.

→>   <←

FEBRUARY 2001

I'm off to the East Village
it's stranger than Mombasa!
I'll burn and kill and pillage,
and bring you a kielbasa!

XXXXX's
Jer

→>   <←

OCTOBER 2003

I'm heading off to Flatbush
a place that's bright and sunny.
Where people with a fat tush
aren't even looked at funny.
Then I'll hurry home again
to see my honey bunny!

XXXXX's
Jer

Sunset Boulevard was, of course, a great movie. In 1995, Andrew Lloyd Webber's musical version of the movie opened on Broadway. The title song's singer pronounced the word "boulevard" in a very strange way. Jerry and lots of other Broadway fans put an unnatural accent on the first syllable of "boulevard" whenever they mentioned the show. Hence the poem below:

APRIL 1995

It's Sixty-fourth and Broadway
and I won't work too hard
I'll ask some simple questions
not like Shakespeare, the Bard.
This show is even easier
than Sunset Boooolevard!

XXXX's
Jer

Jerry's grandfather was a coal miner from Pennsylvania.

➤➤ ◄◄

OCTOBER 1997

No one's at work
no beeper sounds
no steam shovel or tractor,
but who's this guy who's wide awake?
It's Jerry O., the Actor!
I could have been a carpenter
or maybe a designer
Instead I'm leaving in the dark
like Grandpa, the coal miner!

XXXX's
Jer

Richard Belzer and Jerry on the set of Law & Order

➤➤   ◄◄

January 1998

Well, here I go again my love
I'm up to my old tricks.
I'm heading for the pier now.
It's seven thirty-six.
The guys on the construction crew
are playing pick-up sticks!

XXXX's
Jer

➤➤   ◄◄

July 1998

The morning's gray
the sun is red
it's sticky hot and muggy.
My honey's safely in our bed
all cuddly warm and huggy.

But I must go and do a show
past Fifty-third Street's border,
and make obscene amounts of dough
oh good old Law & Order!

XXXX's
Jer

→→   ←←

Thank you for that sweet massage
my back is feeling glorious.
now when I run to catch the crooks
I know I'll be victorious!

XXXXX's
Jer

→>   <←

MARCH 2001

I don't have a poem
'cause I thought you'd awaken.
Now I must leave home
just to bring back the bacon.
But if you think Jerome
would leave you forsaken
I've knocked out this tome
so you're sadly mistaken!

XXXXX's
Jer

→>   <←

NOVEMBER 2001

Some day I'll have a whole day off.
And things will be so rosy!
You'll see me in the light of day,
not like Bela Lugosi!

XXXXX's
Jer

Jerry slipped into the established *Law & Order* ensemble easily. One reason was that Ed Sherin, Jerry's director in the Broadway play *6 Rms Riv Vu*, was *Law & Order's* executive producer. Ed also directed some of the episodes. Jerry and the crew loved working with Ed because he had a marvelous eye and got the shots on one or two takes. And Ed loved Jerry because he was always prepared and had the right coloring and emphasis.

→→   ←←

FEBRUARY 2002

We're filming on the street today
so sayeth the one-liner
the sky is black and I am gray
I feel like a coal miner!
I'll call you in a little bit
you are my one sun-shiner!

It's a quarter to eight
I've been quietly creeping
now I've got to go
while you're peacefully sleeping
I know it's not fun
to read papers alone
but thanks Mr. Bell
for inventing the phone!

It's five fifty-two
there's no one in the place
except me and you—
so stay asleep hon,

you've still got several hours
till you have to run,
but when you get up—
just raise up your cup
and toast to the show—
'cause it's one for my baby
and one more for the dough!

The hunter's going out again
to bring us home the bacon
the most Neanderthal of men
wait for the sun to waken!
Thank you for the lovely note
or should I say love letter.
I'm glad that you sat down and wrote,
and I can do much better!
I love you with all my heart—
you are my life—
nothing else matters.

XXXX's
Jer

Maria Ouspenskaya made a movie where a ballerina injures herself, and Maria says in her Middle European accent, "Get me annuder dencer, dis one broke." Jerry always thought the line was hilarious.

MARCH 1995

Someone got sick
and now we have to work—
is this a joke?
what ever happened to
get me "nudder actress
dis one broke!"

XXXX's
Jer

→→   ←←

JANUARY 1996

I'm sitting in the dark—
all set to film a thriller—

I'm off to Central Park
to catch a dirty killer!
But one thing you must know
but all the stars above you,
the best part of these poems
is saying that I love you!

XXXX's
Jer

→≻   ≺←

JANUARY 1996

I've shaved and balmed
for my complexion,
my hair is blown
to sheer perfection.
There's not a thing
that looks defective,
I'm playing
a New York detective?

XXXX's
Jer

→→   ←←

SEPTEMBER 1996

I wake before the sunlight shines.
I shave with great precision.
Is my job working in the mines?
No! I'm on television!

XXXX's
Jer

Jerry liked Benjamin Bratt from the very beginning of *Law & Order*. Ben was a very intelligent actor and extremely disciplined, even though he was young. Jerry treated Ben like a son and took him under his wing. And Ben, who didn't have a father as a role model, took to Jerry as well. They were inseparable on the set.

It was a loving relationship. Jerry and Ben usually spent their lunch and dinner breaks together . . . and Jerry blamed his growing waistline on Ben's ravenous appetite! Ben loved to eat and would never gain an ounce. He was a young man, a runner and an athlete, and he burned off weight. Jerry was older, and it became harder and harder for him to keep slim. He always complained about Ben's ability to eat anything he wanted and still remain "TV slim."

Ben remembered how intimidating it was to start work on *Law & Order* with the (by that time) legendary Jerry Orbach, especially as a replacement for the beloved Chris Noth . . . and how Jerry made him feel right at home.

The first time I stepped onto the set of Law & Order *back in '95 I was nervous as hell, and everybody knew it. After all, I was the "new guy" replacing Chris Noth as Jerry O's partner in crime fighting, and by all expectations, I had something to prove.*

Now first day, first setup, the routine was to rehearse the scene, give the crew the set for lighting, then come back twenty minutes later to shoot. I hurriedly ran back to my trailer and used that time to go over my lines and do some breathing exercises to try and relax, but it didn't work. When I made my way back to set for one final rehearsal before shooting the scene, I was still a wreck and Jerry O could tell. He shot me a quick, sympathetic smile, then looked down and away, as if to avoid a pending car wreck.

My heart sank. This was it, my moment of truth, my last chance to take a breath and focus just before the director Ed Sherin called "action." The assistant director yelled out "roll camera!" All eyes were on the actors, and Jerry O leaned in to me and slyly said out of the side of his mouth, "You're not really gonna do it that way, are you?" I froze solid, then everybody fell out laughing, including me, and that was the start of a beautiful friendship. Jerry had the good sense to see humor in almost everything, and that's what made him so fun to be around. Yes, he was known as the consummate pro, quick with a joke or a dropped line (he often memorized everyone else's lines, too), but I had the good fortune to know him as a friend, a brother, and at times, a surrogate father. For four seasons we spent nearly every day together, sharing stories, meals, laughs, and even hardships. I used to tease him that I got to have more lunches with him than his adored wife, Elaine. But even if that were true, no one took her place when it came to his admiration.

And Jerry loved a lot of things. He loved to talk shop and tell stories, he loved to sing and play golf, he loved fried calamari and vodka martinis (until the docs said "no"), he loved flamenco music and Sinatra and Celine Dion, he loved reading the newspapers three at a time, he loved the NYT crossword puzzle and finishing with just the "across" clues, he loved hanging out at "the club" and running the table in a game of nine-ball. And Jerry Orbach loved his job. He loved the work, the friends, the camaraderie. But more than all of that, Jerry O loved the beauty of words, and he loved nothing or no one more than Elaine.

In her he found his perfect muse, a red-headed siren in a dancer's body, his heaven-sent match in humor and wit. She inspired him to such a degree that daily, in the wee hours just before sunrise, as the coffee brewed and she quietly slept in the other room, Jerry would write out little love poems or a funny ditty before heading off to work. And sometimes, as a proud young suitor might, he would share the better ones with me at work, just as he would share the ardor he still felt for his wife and best friend, even after all these years.

My dear friend and sister, and the third of our trio of cop musketeers, Epatha Merkerson, used to have a saying whenever we found ourselves chuckling in the presence of Jerry O's immense charm and good fortune. She'd say, "When I grow up, I wanna be Jerry Orbach!"

Having known the man and the way he touched people, I think we all did.

I suggested to Jerry that we try to learn Spanish so we could better communicate with our apartment staff and so he could speak in Spanish with the crew on *Law & Order*. We bought a bunch of cassette tapes, which we played in the car. But Jerry had the advantage. He practiced his Spanish with Ben. They talked back and forth to each other in Spanish and laughed a lot. Jerry's and my bright idea to learn Spanish didn't get very far, but he was able to make fun of his attempts.

→> ←←

SEPTEMBER 2002

The shoes I wear
are not by "Prada"
the dance I do
is not Lambada.
When I kiss you
it's "yada, yada!"
You say thank you?
I say "de nada!"

XXXXX's
Jer

→→   ←←

Buenos dias bonita senora!
Here's a bilingual poem ahora.
Though it's mucho temprano,
and I have no piano—
como esta cosas in Glocca Morra?

XXXX's
Jer

→→   ←←

JULY 1998

Perdon my sweet senora
I'm going to the meeting
I will be back ahora
and kiss you much in greeting!
I'd make a longer verso
but the tiempo, she is fleeting!

XXXX's
Jer

➤➤ ◄◄

AUGUST 1998

I'm off to work but by and by,
I'll be back 'cause I know so.
Just look out at the gorgeous sky,
el dia glorioso!

XXXX's
Jer

➤➤ ◄◄

AUGUST 1998

Sleep well my love
until you rise
and cut up all the "frutas."
Remember, in my loving eyes,
you simply are the "cutas!"

XXXX's
Jer

Jesse Martin, like Ben, was a younger man. Jesse had come to the series after appearing on Broadway in the musical, *Rent*. Since they had musicals in common, when there were down-times on the set Jesse danced and sang, Jerry sang the big notes, and Epatha Merkerson harmonized (Jerry lovingly called her "Eep"). Jesse is a tremendously talented performer.

Jerry with S. Epatha Merkerson and Jesse L. Martin

→>   <←

July 1997

I have to go to work today
so here's a poem to keep.
Jump back in bed and right away
it's no good—five hour's sleep!
But I'm not going to China
Rangoon or Mandalay
I'm near the Empire Diner
just thirty blocks away!

XXXX's
Jer

→>   <←

5:30 in the morning!
Hooray and goody goody!
Oh well, I guess that Streisand's up,
and probably so's Woody.
The "glamour" of a film career
can sometimes leave you wishing,

if I am up this time of day
I should be deep-sea fishing!

XXXX's
Jer

→→   ←←

FEBRUARY 2000

My honey's sleeping peacefully
the sun has not yet risen
the sailor standing watch at sea,
can't see beyond the mizzen
who else is waking up with me?
My crew, and guys in prison!

XXXXX's
Jer

→≻   ≺←

A dark and gloomy Monday
(or so it now appears)
I'm working in the courtroom
(where I haven't been in years)
I'm suffering from
what could become
the strangest of all fears
the booming tones
of James Earl Jones
might hurt my little ears!

XXX's

I love you,
Jer

→→ ←←

Early rising isn't bad
I'm up with lark and whip-poor-will
So don't be scared and don't be sad,
I'll be back soon from Wykagyl!

XXXX's
Jer

Jerry was amazed that *Law & Order* was so popular. It seemed that whenever we went around the dial of our television, there was a rerun of the program.

→→   ←←

APRIL 2002

What happened to that "day of spring"?
I guess we must have missed it
well, suddenly it's summertime
it's useless to resist it.
We'll open up the trunk this week
and put away our flannels,
and then I'll say I love you
on all six hundred channels!

XXXXX's
Jer

Jerry never minded having to do publicity for the show.

MAY 2003

Oh what a busy morning!
Today *and then* The View.
And if it should get boring
a root canal at two!
But it will all be worth it
when I come home to you!

XXXXX's
Jer

→≻ ≺←

I'm going to do Today
then I've got Conan *to do.*
All I need now is a "ta-da!"
and maybe a rim shot or two.
But after the yakking
and press-agent flacking,
I'll come running home to you!

XXXX's
Jer

It seemed like Jerry was nominated for every award but, somehow, because he made it all look easy, he didn't always win.

MARCH 1995

I don't need an "Oscar"
I don't need an "Emmy"
I don't need more "Tonys"
to brighten up my life
'cause I've got a "Lainie"
who'll always be my wife!

XXXX's
Jer

→→   ←←

MARCH 1998

I'd like to thank my wife, Elaine,
for all the things she does.
For lovely dinners, and nose hair trimmers
that whisk away my fuzz.
For all the love that makes each day
a waking thrill for me,
thank God that I don't have to thank
the dumb Academy!

XXXX's
Jer

→→   ←←

FEBRUARY 1999

It's almost time for SAG Awards
the Oscar, and the Emmy.
And I can't win by asking "Who?
When did they leave? How many?"
But I don't care I'll just survive
by being snide and funny
'cause I already got my prize
my lovely honey bunny!

XXXX's
Jer

Married Life

➤➤   ◄◄

WHEN JERRY AND I were first married, I had made my name in the theater and ended up having a career for twenty years. I was hired for anything I really wanted, and there came a time when I didn't have to audition because I was wanted. It was a wonderful time.

A lot of the people I knew and worked with have passed on. It was another time and another world. If I say my first Broadway show was *Fiorello!* some people don't even know who Fiorello La Guardia was, let alone what *Fiorello!* was. To this day many people don't even know that Jerry sang. They only know him from *Dirty Dancing* or the twelve years he had on *Law & Order*. They don't even know he was the voice of Lumiere in Disney's animated film *Beauty and the Beast*.

But while Jerry was working on Broadway or on *Law & Order*, home was where I wanted to be. I kept up with voice lessons and kept in shape, and I have for over thirty years now.

Sure, I was being offered jobs out of town, but being away from Jerry was not an option.

Jerry and I were content to be by ourselves, at our cozy home in New York, without the usual trappings of fame. We didn't have a super fancy car or a driver or a housekeeper. I loved cooking and cleaning the house and watering the plants—things I could never do when I was working. Don't get me wrong, we went out to the SAG and Emmy Award shows, and Jerry had a great time when he sang at the Oscars for *Beauty and the Beast*. And we enjoyed going on cruises when Jerry was the guest celebrity. But we were mostly contented just to be with each other and our beloved kitties, Sammy and Bootsie, which we adopted from one of our favorite charities, Bideawee.

Professionally, Jerry didn't need people taking care of him. He could always do it better. He never had a publicist. As his celebrity grew because of *Law & Order*, he enjoyed the publicity. But having only Saturday and Sundays together, we preferred to just snuggle up with me on the couch in front of the TV rather than have a big night out on the town.

We never owned a home in the city, we rented. We talked about buying a home, but we had a beautiful apartment facing the Hudson River on the 20th floor. Apartment 20A gave us glorious sunsets and was spacious enough for us. Every time we went looking to buy an apartment, something was always in the way of the view; another building or something. We went back to view an apartment a second time and something was amiss, especially after going home and sitting in our apartment and thinking, "We've got a better one." We wanted to stay on the West Side close to his club and Broadway.

We both enjoyed saving, especially me, and we kept waiting for that first million to show up, which was inevitable because we didn't spend on anything. It was such fun to be saving. We both came from a time of life when you just didn't have it. I always had the philosophy, "Save a little. Spend a little." I even saved $15 a week from my $75 a week unemployment check. And we were looking forward to the time when we could retire together and have enough money to do whatever we wanted.

Working on a continuing series forces you to make changes in your life. Before this, Jerry was free most of the day and then walked over to whichever theater he was performing in. Now our schedules became more intricate. On Mondays, Tuesdays, and sometimes Wednesdays, he worked from seven in the morning till as late as eight at night. On those nights when he worked late, I made a lot of one-pot dinners so I could take my portion and keep the rest on the stove for when he came back. I always had to say, "Am I cooking for me or am I cooking for us?" I never knew when he'd be kept overtime. By the time Friday came along, his calls were later and later and sometimes he didn't come home till midnight. He always had the night schedule of the theater in him. He watched the news and then we watched *The Golden Girls* or *Everybody Loves Raymond* until we went to sleep.

We didn't take many vacations prior to *Law & Order*, because we didn't have the money. When Jerry became famous, he was asked by Professor Richard Brown to be a celebrity on cruise ships. We went on major cruises because Jerry was the celebrity, now. The cruise was free. We saw parts of the world that we never would have gone to and in the most elegant fashion. We had a very rich life on these liners.

Jerry in his "cruise bathrobe"

We couldn't go on a cruise the last summer of his life because he was in chemotherapy. We went to Morocco with Robin Leach and his Gourmet Getaways series. How often do you say, "Honey, let's go to Morocco." We stayed at La Mamounia in Marrakech. It was quite luxurious. We came back to New York with fabulous memories and some that were not so hot. While in Morocco, Jerry got violently ill from food poisoning after eating something that tasted great. After his stomach started to rebel, he half jokingly said, "Whatever it's called, it means 'death to the infidel.'" Jerry had to appear on Leach's show and pretend he wasn't green.

But mostly we were content simply to stay in our little apartment, 20A. Life was his work, the golf, his card games with the boys, our vacations, and just being loved and giving love at the same time. We were happy just in being together with someone you loved. It was low key. One of the first things he said to me was, "You made me stop biting my nails." He had a sense of well-being. I wasn't a pushy or needy person, we were just together as a loving couple.

Jerry could have been a professional eater. He didn't necessarily like fancy food, but he did like to eat. When he met Ben Bratt and they started eating together during the filming of *Law & Order*, he was in trouble. As I mentioned, Jerry got sick from the food in Morocco. This poem shows how, after one big meal, he was ready to travel to have more exotic food—as well as a romantic trip to a faraway country.

Jerry and Robin Leach in Morocco

→›   ‹←

I'm sorry for these hours
that keep me out of sight
(I'm sorry that I ate so much
at Passover last night!)
but soon's a nice long weekend
and I long to press your flesh
and I think of this, it won't be long
til we're in Marrakech!

XXXX's
Jer

Here's another tribute to Jerry's capacity for eating, especially when we went to a friend's house for Passover.

→→   ←←

The brisket and the horseradish,
the kugel and the peas,
the macaroons and slivovitz
have dropped me to my knees.
So after gaining so much weight
it makes me stop and wonder,
do Jews "Pass over" Heaven's gate
or do they just pass under?

XXXXX's
Jer

→→   ←←

JUNE 1995

I'm ready to go
it's twenty past eight
time for me to leave home.
I know you're awake
but pretending to sleep
just so I'll write you a poem!

XXX
Jer

Jerry wrote me a poem about every facet of our lives together. Here's a poem about our early morning routine.

DECEMBER 2001

The papers, the coffee
the yogurt, the fruit . . .
the simple little pleasures,
the things I like to do.
They're transformed into treasures
by doing them with you!

XXXXX's
Jer

Jerry was always concerned about me and always wanted to protect me.

→≻   ≺←

MAY 2001

I hope more sleep has come to you
and that you're feeling better.
I guess the only thing to do
is put more kisses on your letter!

XXXXXXXXX's
Jer

→≻   ≺←

SEPTEMBER 1996

You said, "Don't write a poem today."
But I am writing anyway.
There's not enough time in the day
to say the things I want to say.
A million poems my whole life through,
could never tell my love for you!

XXX's
Jer

Joan Hamburg had a very successful radio career in New York City. I once replaced her on Arthur Schwartz's radio show.

MARCH 2003

My honey on the radio!
It's like a month of Sundays.
have fun and tell 'em what you know,
and be sure to wear clean undies!

XXXXX's
Jer

Jerry loved to stay up late at night despite the fact that he had to get up early in the morning. After all the years on Broadway, he had an actor's schedule—going to sleep around two in the morning and waking around 11 a.m. I would try not to nag him to go to sleep, but I knew the next day's work would be hard if he didn't get enough sleep.

→➤ ⊰←

I'm sorry I was dumb last night
(What gets into my head?)
you shouldn't have to fuss and fight
to make me go to bed!
I will be better and have some sense
and listen from now on.
To sit there's really kind of dense
not watching what isn't on!

XXXX's
Jer

→>—   —<←

NOVEMBER 1994

That scotch and milk
sure did the trick
I went to sleep
and double quick!
It could become a nightly habit
cooked up by such a lovely wabbit!

XXXX's
Jer

Because Jerry had trouble falling to sleep, we had a white-noise machine in the bedroom. One night he was having a particularly difficult time. I turned to him and soothingly said, "Honey, listen to the sound . . ." And then I paused and sang, "of the men working on the chain gang." He cracked up. That snapped him out of his insomnia and let him relax enough to fall asleep. The next day, Jerry wrote this poem to me.

➤➤ ◄◄

JANUARY 1996

The dawn doth break
across the sky —
the sun is up, and so am I!
The nice thing about rising early,
is writing poems to my girlie!
(Listen to the sound . . .
of the men . . .)

XXXX's
Jer

Our love nest, apartment 20A, figured in many of Jerry's poems to me.

→→   ←←

Although I work too early,
I guess I shouldn't bitch.
'Cause think of what they pay me,
we're piling up the gold.
But answer me a riddle—
why ain't the water cold?

→→   ←←

The wind is mild
the sky is blue
and soon I will be kissing you
but all's not perfect,
here's the rub—
there's a sweater
in my tub!

→→   ←←

It's now the end of April.
I'm shivering and wheezing.
I wish it was December,
'cause this apartment's freezing!
I hope this poem has warmed you up
and that you find me pleasing!

→→   ←←

I know you're gonna get up soon
'cause there won't be no water.
Oh well, you could be Esther Williams
doing Neptune's Daughter.
Or even worse, imagine if—
you were a lady otter!

XXXXX's
Jer

→>-   -<←

SEPTEMBER 1998

It's dark out,
but I'll make my deadline
in fact, I'm even early
the president's in every headline
I'm feeling hurt and surly.
But all the nasty things they preach us
soon will go away and even hurricanes can't
    reach us
here in 20A!

XXXX's
Jer

→→   ←←

APRIL 1999

It's 6:26, but I'm not bitchin'
'cause it looks like beautiful weather.
When I come home,
We'll sit in the kitchen
and stare at the tofu together!

XXXXX's
Jer

We had been discussing painting the apartment and couldn't settle on a color. Jerry managed to slip in some of his political feelings in this poem.

NOVEMBER 2000

A dark and rainy morning
it looks like deepest night.
But I don't mind the darkness,
our kitchen's nice and bright!
We'll paint another color too,

so please don't let that trouble ya.
The thing we have to suffer through
is four years of George Dubblya!

XXXXXX's
Jer

Jerry was a good-bye kisser and a hello kisser and a between-commercials kisser. And because I was five-foot-two and he was six-foot-one or six-foot-two, I would get a stiff neck. I had this old upholstered footstool, and whenever we wanted to kiss I would stand on it to make it easier for our lips to meet. So whenever we wanted to hug and kiss, he'd say, "Get on the kissing stool" so we could be nose to nose and I could get hugs and kisses. After Jerry's death, when I left 20A for my new apartment, I just couldn't throw it out, even though it doesn't go with my new apartment's decor.

AUGUST 2000

I'm off to work in Newark!
(Not just around the block.)
I haven't worked in Newark
since I did summer stock!

But I'll be back this evening
with many tales to tell.
And stand you on the kissing stool
and hug you till you yell!

XXXXX's
Jer

The Gowanus Canal in Brooklyn is known throughout New York City as a particularly revolting body of polluted water.

SEPTEMBER 2000

September 21 my love
and autumn is upon us.
To reach you at the kissing stool
I'd swim the foul Gowanus!

XXXXX's
Jer

I stood so often on the kissing stool, the padding was wearing out.

JULY 2001

A glorious day in this neighborhood
it's sunny, clear and cool!
I am so happy you're my queen
I'll gladly be your fool!
But if I want some lovin'
I must fix the kissing stool!

XXXXX's
Jer

→> <←

NOVEMBER 1994

The traffic's starting early
the sky is bright above
in the next room is my girlie,
the lady I love!
Ooh! I gotta go!
But wooh! I love you so!

XXXX's
Jer

Jerry *and* Elaine Orbach

AUGUST 1994

This poem is like a letter
to read when you awake.
I hope your fingers are better
and that your head don't ache,
I hope today is sunny
and skies are pollen-free
and no one tries anything funny
'cause you belong to me!

XXX's
Jer

→⤚　⤙←

AUGUST 1995

6 a.m. Not the best of times,
for making up these brilliant rhymes,
so I'll be sweet
instead of clever—
and say our love
will last forever!

XXXX's
Jer

→⤚　⤙←

NOVEMBER 1995

I envisioned herds of antelope
and hippos in the streams.
A monkey eating cantaloupe
beneath the moon's pale beams.
But nothing, not a cockatoo,

or panda bear it seems,
can ever quite compare to you—
the one gorilla my dreams!

XXXXX's
Jer

→> <←

MARCH 1996

"Let's kill all the lawyers!"
What Shakespeare said is true.
But, if they hurt my honey,
Let's kill the dentists too!
Pain, pain, go away
my honey cuts her hair today.
I Love You—

XXXX's
Jer

➤➤ ◄◄

APRIL 1996

Although my call is later
and I guess you'll be awake,
that don't mean I can't write
some poetry for goodness' sake!
I don't write all these poems
just simply to be clever.
Each one is like a song that says
our love will last forever!

XXXX's
Jer

➤➤ ◄◄

JULY 1996

My hair is combed
my teeth are pearly
I find I'm fifteen minutes early!
I write these poems

to make you chuckle
if you're the belt, then I'm the buckle,
if you're the berry, I'm the huckle
if I don't stop I'll . . .

XXXX's
Jer

→→   ←←

OCTOBER 1996

Guten Morgen Sweety-Hertzen
das sun is upf-gereisin!
Here is ein German Vertzen
now ist das nich surpreisin?
I love you
(in any language)

XXXX's
Jer

➤➤   ◄◄

DECEMBER 1996

Tomorrow you're my valentine
but what about today?
An ordinary Thursday
and I'm working far away.
And will I love you Arbor Day?
And what about St. Swivens?
And how about Robin Givens?
(nothing else rhymed)
Okay, it's time to end this poem,
enough of being clever.
Thing is, I love you every day,
and that goes on forever!

XXXXX's
Jer

Jerry *and* Elaine Orbach

➤➤   ◄◄

AUGUST 1997

Without you I'm a one-winged bird.
A ship without a rudder.
A baseball player left on third,
A fadder with no mudder.
A wandering bum
A lonesome dove.
I'm golf without a caddy!
You'll always be my one true love
I love you, Uncle Daddy.

Once in a while, Jerry had writer's block when trying to think up a poem.

JULY 1994

I can't think of a poem today,
(That pencil was too light!)
so I'll just scribble anyway,
'cause you'll read what I write.
As you go on your merry way

and someone bumps or shoves you
remember back in 20A,
there is a guy who loves you!

→> <←

SEPTEMBER 2000

Some days no poem comes flowing out
my mind's a total blank.
But I love you without a doubt,
so take that to the bank!

If I can't make a poem today
they'll drop me from the rhymers!
Thank God this ditty came my way
I thought I had Alzheimer's!

→> <←

MARCH 2001

My head is full of stuffing
I cannot find a rhyme!

I can't come up with nuffing
I haven't got the time!
Well that's enough of bluffing
I'm stopping on a dime!
(Our love is still sublime!)

Jerry's Love Affair
with New York

→→   ←←

*J*ERRY WAS BORN IN the Bronx, but his family moved away shortly thereafter—he couldn't wait to get back. After he dropped out of college to attend the Actors Studio, the leading acting school in New York City, he never considered leaving again. He owed it a lot for his career from the very beginning. Hollywood never treated him as well as New York did.

As for me, I came from Pittsfield, Massachusetts, and got my first Broadway show at nineteen. I never thought about leaving either. And it also gave me my life and career . . . and bunions. My great friend Millicent Martin always said to me, "Those feet gave you your career. You earned those bunions by dancing in those shoes."

Jerry loved the pulse, the people, the grit of New York, and being able to buy a paper on the corner or a carton of milk whenever he wanted. We never even wanted a country house because our apartment in New York gave us everything we wanted in a home. Our apartment was the center of our New York world. When we were married and living on Fifty-third Street, we were a block from Jerry's gym, the Lone Star Boat Club, and just three blocks from the Winter Garden Theatre where Jerry was starring in the musical *42nd Street*. He barely took off his makeup before walking home to me and our apartment.

New York isn't a warm and fuzzy place. We always felt the warmer and fuzzier a town is, the slower life is. There is always a love/hate thing with this city, and Jerry and I loved to go on vacation but we loved it even more when we returned home.

The citizens of New York were great to us. The success of *Law & Order* and the charity work Jerry did for the police department meant that the cops at the Midtown North precinct station waved to him on the street. One policeman said to him, "Keep making us look good." Once when it was pouring rain and we couldn't get a cab or a bus, a police car drove up and the driver yelled out, "Hey Jer, get in. Where you going? We'll give you a ride." As we climbed into the backseat, I couldn't help but joke, "I hope nobody sees us getting into this police car."

Tourists, truck drivers, and other New Yorkers would always yell out, "Hey Jerry." But when we were out eating at our neighborhood restaurant, Da Tomasso, nobody bothered us. The only thing that bothered Jerry was when people would come up to him and tell him how much they loved him on *L.A. Law*. Finally, he became so well established via *Law & Order*, people never confused the shows—though there were a few people who claimed to love him on *NYPD Blue*.

At Jerry's memorial service, Mayor Michael Bloomberg spoke of Jerry's value to New York. "For New Yorkers, there was something wonderfully familiar about Detective Briscoe—irascible, intelligent, and with enough one-liners to fill a Centre Street holding cell. Briscoe exuded the life of the city and all its moxie, but peel back those layers of cynicism and you'll find a character with tremendous integrity and the intent to do the best job that he could.

"Jerry's nuanced portrayal of Detective Briscoe became the admirable face of the NYPD, and Jerry came to personify New York in both body and soul to so many people around this country. As Jerry said of New York, 'I live it, I love it, and I represent it.'

"Jerry truly cared for this city just as the city truly cared for him. Jerry Orbach was a New York original. He was a quintessential New York actor and someone who deserves to be remembered as a true prince of the city."

Jerry gave back to New York through his celebrity. He hosted benefits for Bideawee, North Shore Animal League, celebrity golf tournaments, the Brooklyn Academy of Music, and the New York City Opera among others. He was asked by Jackie Onassis to help save Grand Central Terminal because he was a theater celebrity. We also gave to charities monetarily, but his name was more valuable to the charities because he would bring in celebrities and people with deep pockets.

Through his work on *Law & Order*, with his character of Lennie Briscoe, Jerry became a symbol of New York. Mayors Giuliani and Bloomberg acknowledged his importance to the city. Jerry and Sam Waterston were named Living Landmarks of New York by the Landmarks Conservancy. Jerry quipped, "You know what that means, they can never tear us down."

JANUARY 1994

The steam pipes are whining
the sun's not yet shining
but wait, what's that heavenly glow?
It's still really night out!
we're buried in masses,
right up to our asses
in vodee-o-dodee-o snow!

→→   ←←

JANUARY 1994

It's six o'clock
the land is dark—
they've even closed the bars.
The only schmucks who venture out
are night watchmen, bus drivers
muggers and TV Stars!

Alan Jay Lerner and Frederick Loewe wrote a popular musical, *Brigadoon*, about a Scottish town that only appears for one day every one hundred years.

DECEMBER 1995

The fog is here—white-out complete.
Can't see the cars down on the street.
There ain't no sun there ain't no moon
New Jersey could be Brigadoon!
But while I'm off at work or play
one thing will see me through the day.

When I come home from making money,
I'm gonna hug my honey bunny!

→>   <←

JANUARY 1998

Some day the sun will shine again
upon the cliffs of Dover.
The buzz bombs will not whine again,
the war will soon be over.
But wait, those are the Palisades!
I think I see Hoboken!
My nightmare slowly, slowly fades,
I'm glad I have awoken!

>> <<

JUNE 1998

Living in this city
can toughen up your brain,
the heat, the noise, the sirens
the dirty subway train,
the TV nominations
don't give me any pain,
hey, I don't need an Emmy,
'cause I've got my Elaine!

In Riverdale or Inwood
Or far Hoboken, too.
The natives always worship
the way that I love you!
(You were gorgeous last night.)

New York, New York at 6 a.m.
The leader of the nation!
No rooster crows,
no robin sings
in sunrise celebration.

But beeper horns and squeaky brakes,
what is this strange sensation?
Well bless my luck, the faithful truck—
Dept. of Sanitation!

Being a voracious reader and quite smart, Jerry got all the New York daily newspapers delivered to the apartment. The one he seemed to like the best was Long Island's *Newsday*.

NOVEMBER 2001

No time to write a fancy poem,
so I'll just grab my Newsday
I've got to run
I love you hon,
and it's election Tuesday!

→→　←←

FEBRUARY 2002

6:30 on a Tuesday
a lovely springlike day.
I hope I get my Newsday
before I go away.
It really doesn't matter
there's not much that is new!
The only thing important is
you love me, I love you.

→→ ←←

SEPTEMBER 2003

Calloo callay a lovely day!
I just brought in the Newsday.
I love you, but I must go away
so have a lovely Tuesday!

Jerry at his desk, papers at hand

→>   <←

AUGUST 2002

"Lots lemon" yogurt
rhymes with Humphrey Bogurt.
My Long Island Newsday
only rhymes with Tuesday.
No one but Paul Anka
rhymes with Casablanca.
But it's plain to see
that you rhymes with me!

He also read weekly *Variety*, the show business newspaper.

AUGUST 2003

My poem is running late today
it's causing high anxiety,
the reason that I got this way?
I had to read Variety!

→>   <+-

DECEMBER 2003

It's not much of a poem today,
(got stuck reading Variety*).*
But I still feel the same old way,
I love you high and miety!

→>   <+-

FEBRUARY 2004

I ran a little late today
and didn't read Variety.
So you must bring me up to date
on our show biz society!

More Life with Jerry

->>   -<-

I THOUGHT EVERYBODY HAD A marriage like ours. Marriage is being kind and respectful to each other. You have your little tiffs but not enough to hurt somebody, ever. This isn't to say that we didn't have any conflicts, of course. Coming from an Italian background, I have a temper and can get frustrated easily at a situation that is out of my control. Looking back, I have no idea why my frustration took over my logic, especially with Jerry. I was usually angry at some extraneous thing, not the real reason for my impatience. I always knew when I went too far and was too crazy or out of control. If Jerry's tone of voice went one notch up I knew I had crossed the line. It wasn't what Jerry said—it was his tone of voice. I immediately pulled back. And usually he was right. I saw things differently.

He never wanted to be a bad guy, and that also made me frustrated on his behalf. He'd just smile at me and say, "It's all right." I can remember when I would get very upset and angry and I'd hold back my emotions until I thought I'd explode. And Jerry would say, "Come here, honey." And I would say, "Don't hug me. Don't hug me. I'll cry and I can't cry." And he would say to me over and over again with that smile on his face and his eyes all twinkly, "You little toughy," until I would break and laugh.

On the weekends things had to be done around the house. When I hurt my back he wanted to do the vacuuming. I would be his "cord girl." He'd say, "Come on, cord girl, pick up the cord." We would go around the apartment together with him pushing the machine and me following with the cord. On the hot summer days he would be in his boxers vacuuming. That was hilarious, the big television star in his shorts pushing the vacuum with me following behind holding the cord.

APRIL 1998

I know that you can't eat or drink,
so here's what you can do—
make phone calls, put your makeup on,
and do the laundry too!
For many years you "scanned" our cats,
now let those cats scan you!

When I hurt my back not only did I get out of vacuuming, I also didn't have to do the laundry. Jerry dutifully and gladly took the basket of laundry along with the bottles of detergent and quarters for the machines and went down to our laundry room in our building's basement. En route he'd run into some of the wives who lived in the apartment house, and they'd say, "Hey, Jerry what are you doing laundry for?" He'd shrug and not make a big deal out of it.

Well, one day he was coming back from work and got on the elevator. In the elevator was one of the husbands who lived in the building. He backed Jerry into a corner of the elevator and told him that his wife berated him. "What are you doing?" he asked Jerry, "My wife keeps saying, 'If Jerry Orbach can do the laundry, you can too!'"

Here's proof that Jerry Orbach, star of stage and screen, took our laundry and a bunch of quarters downstairs to the laundry room and did our laundry.

> *Oops! I'm running out of undies!*
> *One too many travel Sundays.*
> *I know the way to end this quandary,*
> *Tomorrow I will do the laundry!*

> *XXXXX's*
> *Jer*

Jerry was not a picky eater. I cooked him all the peasant Italian dishes that are always the best. It was the healthiest diet. There were lots of variations of pasta at least once a week—red sauces, vegetable sauces, and oil and garlic. My Italian dishes were always a mainstay. The only food he wasn't too crazy about was okra. He and I both hated okra—that's one of the things we both shared! Jerry was a good eater and I always wanted to please him. That's where I got the applause, never mind on the stage but in the kitchen. If something didn't come out right, I would be so upset and he'd say, "No, honey, it's great . . . it's just a little . . . no, it's great!"

I did the cooking of dinners, but if there was any meal that he loved to cook it was the breakfast. He made great omelets, and he wanted his bacon cooked crisp but not too crisp. His favorite was scrambled eggs with cottage cheese. He loved cottage cheese folded into the eggs. It was his comfort food. He always timed out the breakfast, "Pop the toast! Where's the paper towels for the bacon?" And when I took too much time buttering the toast he'd say, "Schmear the toast—what are you doing, making a painting?" That came from his father teaching the cooks at Neisner's counter. "You don't have to hit all the corners, just schmear it on."

Jerry always had simple tastes in food.

OCTOBER 2002

Your potato salad was superb,
the dancing was sublime.
But my ride's out there at the curb,
and I must be on time.
I'll call you in a little while
(cops say "I'll drop a dime").

➤➤   ◄◄

AUGUST 1996

You cleaned my lovely bathroom
you tucked me into bed
you gave me turkey hot dogs,
(You cut up my rye bread!)
was ever there a woman
so saved a husband's life
my angel, my beloved,
my lambie-pie, my wife!

XXX's
Jer

Jerry loved Key lime pie.

FEBRUARY 1997

I know we said "No poem today"
but I woke up so early,
I thought I'd write one anyway
because you are my girlie!

I'll love you till the day I die!
till quarter past forever!
I love you more than key lime pie!
Oops! Guess I got too clever!

XXXX's
Jer

→→   ←←

I saw three little donuts,
their holes were very small.
But they caused me to go nuts,
and now there's none at all!

XXXXX's
Jer

We also had a ritual on either Saturday or Sunday of changing the sheets on our king-size bed. We had quite a dance going. It was totally choreographed. We made the bed in no time flat. We loved cold and crisp, clean sheets.

Jerry loved playing golf during his hiatus from filming *Law & Order*. All the golf courses near New York City are on Long

Island or in Westchester County, north of New York City, so he had to leave before breakfast to make tee time. I remember one time he said to me, "Forgive me . . . but I love you because you let me go."

I wasn't a golfer. A city girl needs wheels to get out there and spend eight hours a day practicing. I never had the drive, so to speak. Still, I love golf courses because they're so soothing and so beautiful and pristine. I'd love looking at the wildlife, never mind the balls—I can't see that far anyway. I watched the geese.

Golf was a way of being together on those days that I had nothing pending and he was going away, because that's what he did on his days off. He loved it so much and I'd say I'd come. If he drove the golf cart, being the kind of driver that he was, I bounced all over the cart. He might have gotten us to the next hole quicker, but at least I remained intact if I drove it. I hit my head on the roof a lot. I'd say, "Whoa. Honey, honey, wait a minute!" I drove the cart because I could see what was coming up ahead on the path. And I didn't get a concussion. Even if he had buddies to play with, we got our own cart.

He said to me, "Practice your putting." And I had a good eye. I wanted to be with him and share the beauty of wonderful golf courses and give him encouragement. He hit the ball and asked me, "Where'd the ball go?" and I couldn't see it. I'd say, "It's in the woods over there somewhere." We spent a lot of time searching for lost balls. Just when Jerry was in full swing on the course, the season's filming hiatus ended, and he'd have to recommence work. Come the following April he was rusty all over again!

Jerry on the links

Jerry wrote a number of poems about golf that show just how much he loved the game.

The sun doth shine
the wind doth blow
and so a golfing I will go!
I won't be golfing every day,
although I know it seems that way.
One thing that makes me love you so,
with all my guilt
you let me go!

XXXX's
Jer

June 1995

You deserve a poem today
since I got up and snuck away
I love you more than I can say
how come wolf
doesn't rhyme with golf?

XXXX's
Jer

→→ ←←

AUGUST 1995

I'm clean and dressed
my pants are pressed
(I look just like a wolf.)
where am I going all sharped up?
I'm going to play golf!
(No wonder English is so hard!)

XXXX's
Jer

In the summer, the casts of Broadway shows have a base-ball league. During the winter, the Broadway Show League sponsors a bowling tournament. Although we weren't in a Broadway show, Jerry and I bowled with them. It was great fun as well as exercise and enabled Jerry to still feel part of the world of the theater.

→→   ←←

FEBRUARY 1996

It's six o'clock, the moon is full,
I'm dressed in wool and leather.
Our bed has a magnetic pull
but I'll go face the weather.
I love you so, I hate to leave
but now I must get rolling.
The only thing I can't believe
is that we're going bowling!

XXXX's
Jer

Jerry, as I mentioned earlier, hated winter with a passion (especially since that's when all his outdoor scenes in *Law & Order* seemed to be filmed)! Here are a few of his odes to spring.

→→   ←←

MARCH 2001

I woke with grace,
I shaved my face
my hair is sheer perfection.
Let's laugh and sing
for surely spring
is heading our direction!
(Who is this grace?)

→→   ←←

APRIL 2002

I didn't write a sonnet
about your Easter bonnet.
I didn't write a haiku
to show how much I laiku.
But here's a little jingle
'cause you still make me tingle!

➤➤   ◄◄

APRIL 2002

The sky's polluted up above
a heat inversion's forming.
But nothing's hotter than our love,
not even global warming!

XXXXX's
Jer

➤➤   ◄◄

SEPTEMBER 1999

I woke up at 6:30,
so dark you'd never miss me.
But then my day was brightened,
you woke up just to kiss me!

→→   ←←

OCTOBER 1999

The sun is up!
The sky is blue!
My honey's in the covers!
I wish that i could go there, too,
and we'd be snuggly lovers!

XXXX's
Jer

→→   ←←

JANUARY 2000

It's January, double "O"
long time till spring is sprung.
But why is my heart leaping so?
You are my egg foo young!

XXXX's
Jer

JANUARY 2000

I love my snookey ookums,
though the streets are cold and slushy.
Did I say snookey ookums?
I'm too old to be so gushy!

XXXX's
Jer

→→   ←←

MARCH 2000

'Tis springtime, see the sun's bright rays,
the breeze is wafting o'er us.
And if you sing a song of praise
I'll join you on the chorus.
In some far lands, a poem this bad
would be grounds for divorus!

XXXXX's
Jer

→→   ←←

AUGUST 2000

It isn't going to rain today
no matter what's predicted
so go on out and run and play,
your freedom's unrestricted.
No Burberry's no L.L. Beans
umbrellas or Aquascutums.

So you'll look sweet in blouse and jeans
I love my little cute-ums!

XXXXX's
Jer

→→   ←←

You are my Easter bunny
you make me dance and sing.
The cloudy days feel sunny
you are my breath of spring.
You're also pretty funny,
the most important thing!

XXXXX's
Jer

I can still hear Jerry say the word "poltroon" like W. C. Fields.

> *Tho' I'm a knave, a flim-flam man,*
> *a poltroon and a varlet,*
> *my love for you is deeper than*
> *the love of Rhett for Scarlett!*

> *XXXXX's*
> *Jer*

→→   ←←

SEPTEMBER 2002

> *It's my belief my poem is brief*
> *because I'm running latish.*
> *So here's a kiss, and I'll say this*
> *baby, you're the greatish!*

➤➤   ◄◄

NOVEMBER 2002

Good morning little lambie,
I hope you slept quite soundly.
Now here's the double whammy,
I love you most profoundly!

➤➤   ◄◄

SEPTEMBER 2003

I know there are many rhymes
as there are stars above you,
but I'll just say it three more times,
I love you, I love you, I love you!

→> <←

FEBRUARY 2004

Good morning my sweet valentine,
I hope your sleep was tranquil.
There's no love great as yours and mine
a bushel and a tankfull!
(Close but no rhyme)

→> <←

FEBRUARY 2004

I love your hair, your face, your knees
your shoulders and your bottom.
I know there's more to you than these,
but I'm sure glad you've got 'em!!

→> <←

FEBRUARY 2004

There's not much time to rhyme today,
I'm running kind of latish.
But as Ralph Kramden used to say,
baby, you're the greatish!

There's the VIP and the MVP.
There's RSVP and the Robert E. Lee
but There's Only One MIP.
The Most Important Person in the world to
    me.
I love you, I need you like the roses need rain
but some nights these feelings are hard to
    explain.
Without you I would just be an old
    "Umbriago."
Asleep in the middle of Doctor Zhivago.

Jerry's schedule could be quite exhausting. That's one reason why we so looked forward to vacations. The other reason was that we could spend twenty-four hours with each other and not just in the evenings and on weekends.

> *I know you told me not to write*
> *unless I was inspired.*
> *But I slept pretty well last night*
> *and I'm not feeling tired.*
> *So count the days from one to three,*
> *then start the celebration.*
> *There's Tuesday, Wednesday, Thursday,*
> *and then we're on vacation!*

April 1995

> *I'm going to work now*
> *seven more days and counting,*
> *'twill soon be vacation,*
> *the tension is mounting.*
> *Let's go to the Plaza*
> *and wade in the founting!*

Every year, whether we liked it or not, we had our birthdays. But like most things in life, Jerry took the advancing years with his typical good cheer.

OCTOBER 1994

It's rainy and misty
the wind she is blowing
though I'm almost "sisty"
I got to get going!
I can't think of rhyming
'cause it's seven fifty
and I've lost my timing
since my fifty-ninth bifday!

⇥   ⇤

OCTOBER 1997

I'm sixty-two for goodness' sake,
to say it sure feels funny.
The candles for my birthday cake
would cost a ton of money!
But I feel, maybe, twenty-five

my outlook's bright and sunny.
What makes me glad to be alive?
I got my honey bunny!

→→   ←←

OCTOBER 1998

Thank you for the party
and thank you for the cake.
Thank you for the shoulder bag,
but there must be a mistake.
I can't be sixty-three today
you make me feel so fine
just like Jack Benny used to say,
I'm only thirty-nine!

Anniversaries were a good subject for poems. Here are my favorites.

OCTOBER 1995

I'm tired, but I'll still go to work
I guess I'm really mercenary!
But just once more
I must encore
Happy Anniverserary!

XXXX's
Jer

➤➤   ◄◄

OCTOBER 1996

It's 7:30 I'm such a jerk,
am I playing golf
or going to work?
Forget kindergarten

I belong in the nursery.
oh well, tomorrow's our anniversary!

XXXXX's
Jer

Here's one he wrote for our anniversary in 1997.

One rose for every year with you
is not enough to pay.
Now, what I'd really like to do
is one for every day.
I'd fill the place with fragrance
to show you what my heart meant,
but we'd turn into vagrants
Looking for a new apartment!

XXXX's
Jer

This is his last anniversary poem to me.

OCTOBER 2004

We didn't dance on the night we were wed
we watched some TV, had a drink, went to
    bed.
Out in L.A. we were stuck for a while
we got thru each day with a song and a smile.
Prince of the City *brought us back home*
then 42nd St. *no need to roam*
at last, L&O, *with timing supreme*
it helped us achieve our dream.
So now, here we are, celebrating today.
It's hard to believe how the time slips away.
Twenty-five years, but we don't feel so old.
We've made it to silver
let's go for the gold!

Love,
Jer

Jerry's Illness

➤➤   ◄◄

TWO YEARS INTO *Law & Order*, we were slapped with, "Not so cocky, you." Jerry had gone for his yearly checkup and a couple of days later our family doctor informed us that Jerry's PSA number was a five. It was supposed to be a two. PSA stands for prostate specific antigen, something that is in men's blood and that doctors use to screen for prostate cancer. For two weeks the doctor treated him as if he just had some sort of bug in his prostate. Then he retook the numbers and they had gone up dramatically. That's when Jerry went to a urologist. And that's when these horrendous tests had to be done that were extremely uncomfortable and painful. Jerry was a very strong man and a fighter, but he said he saw stars.

Jerry had prostate cancer and it was the shock of the world to us. It was the very first time we cried together. He wanted life, and he was told to live a full life since prostate cancer is usually a slow-growing disease. Because it was contained, Jerry went for the radiation treatment instead of having his prostate removed. Meanwhile, he worked every day. The radiation treatment was a success, and after the final days of his radiation treatment everyone at *Law & Order* applauded him and gave him a diploma. Jerry's doctor told us, "Go have a great life and come back in six months. There should be nothing." But there was something. And that's when our lives really changed because that's when he had to go through hormonal therapy. It was scary. It was very scary. But we were both pillars of strength in all of this. Of course, in trying to be strong I developed high blood pressure that nobody, not even Jerry, knew about.

The diagnosis that the cancer had metastasized was frightening enough. Living it became a daily routine. But Jerry was determined to be professional and diligent about his treatments. He did everything that they told him he should do, and he did it to the letter. He was the best possible patient, despite the fact that the hormonal therapy would change his male potency. His hair would fall out. He had to get radiation on his pecs so he wouldn't develop breasts. Basically, he was on an estrogen routine. On the first day of therapy he calmly said, "Honey, would you bring me some water?" I brought it to him, and my hand was shaking. He took it, being the good drinker that he was, took the pill, and said, *"L'chaim!"* And that's how he dealt with it for the next ten years. There was a lot of laughter because I believe we made friends with this devil, because we strongly believed the cancer wasn't going to win. Jerry had a good ten years. He shouldn't have had the last five because there were bad things happening. His attitude and his work ethic made a difference.

Most of the people on *Law & Order* knew about the cancer and his treatments. His driver had to take him to the hospital for his radiation before or after work. But nobody at work ever spilled the beans. That shows how much he was loved and respected. The story could have been sold to the supermarket tabloids for a lot of money. The cast and crew loved him for all those years and I loved them for loving him.

Jerry's going-away cake at Law & Order

Every day we lived with "Did you pack your whities?" In the course of the ten years the color of the pills changed from whities to pinkies to greenies to blueies because the strength of the medicine had to be changed as the PSA numbers went up. Thank God they had the medicine to give him. It was an everyday event, just like brushing your teeth or taking vitamins. Jerry was never really ill with this. He was strong enough to deal with it physically and emotionally.

When the cancer learned how to fight the pills, Jerry decided to cut back on his job. He was sixty-eight years old and producer Dick Wolf always said that Jerry could have whatever he wanted. So, Jerry was written out of *Law & Order* and the daily grind. It was very hard for Jerry to say good-bye because that's when he had to start his chemotherapy. But he did it with a smile. He felt he was doing okay as long as his hair stayed in; that's what he used as a benchmark. Of course, he didn't know that when he woke up in the morning, I would take the hair off his pillow with a lint brush.

I knew he knew that he was in bad shape at that point. He kept up his daily routine. He went to the gym to keep strong, he was doing his chemo every day and still went to play golf in the summer. When he came back to 20A, I asked him how he did and he'd say, "I was there. Not up to my usual game but I was there walking the course." I could tell that he was weakening and tired. More than ever, he started to lie down on the couch to take a nap. And then something very bad started happening. We didn't know it but there was a tumor growing on his vocal chords. He started losing his voice, which is a tragedy for any actor or singer. When the new *Law & Order* series, *Trial by Jury*, started, the chords weren't meeting properly. And I was always saying to him, "Honey, clear your throat." But he couldn't shake it off. In the course of filming those first three episodes it was getting worse. One day he couldn't project and the sound man kept saying, "I can't hear him." I don't know if Jerry realized what was happening. The director protected Jerry by changing the tone of the scene. He instructed all the actors to whisper so nobody around the squad room could hear them. And nobody watching the scene on television would know that anything was wrong with Jerry's voice.

Jerry was protecting me and would never tell me what was happening on the set. I knew what was happening at home, but I didn't know how his work was going. One day we were having our coffee when the phone rang. It was Jerry's makeup girl asking how Jerry was doing. I said, "He's fine. Why?" And she said, "He fell on the set yesterday." He got caught on something and couldn't catch himself. They asked if he wanted to stop. He said, "Just give me five minutes." His hair and makeup ladies gave him cold cloths, and five minutes later he was back on the set and said, "Let's go," and finished the scene. I never knew any of this because he had come home and said, "I'm going to lie down," while I was fixing dinner. That phone call broke my heart. I asked him, "Why didn't you tell me?" And he said, "I don't ever want to frighten you." And I replied, "Honey, I'm going through this with you." It was the beginning of the end.

When Jerry was too ill to continue with the series, the cast, crew, and production staff gave him a farewell party. I have a picture of the crew giving him a cake. Jerry is there receiving all this love from them. I am so aware that in the photo Jerry has his hands in his pockets, which means to me, "I'm holding on to my emotional being right now because if I let down, I'm going to cry." I never saw him with his hands in his pockets.

Soon tumors were discovered throughout his body, and they couldn't be stopped. Jerry went through hell in the hospital with many horribly painful treatments. Then there were these interns that came in every day all gloomy and sad. They created a pall in the room. I kicked them out, telling them, "Don't ever come back. There is no gray in this room, there's only sunshine." Jerry loved it and told all the nurses, "You should have heard her this morning." He was so proud of me.

Everyone in the hospital loved him and he kept the nurses laughing. He really fought and fought and fought until the very end. Even when the pills that he thought were helping didn't work anymore, he still wanted to take them. When he took to his bed in Sloan-Kettering, more often than not, he couldn't talk. He was whispering and it was frustrating to him. So I went down to the gift store and looked for something that made noise. It was Christmastime and there was a little Mrs. Santa Claus that had a bell under her skirt. I told him, "Honey, when you want me after you wake up, ring the bell." After he passed, I immediately threw that away.

They finally put him in a coma so he wouldn't feel any pain. It was so hard to see him lying there. That was the hardest part, knowing that he wasn't there. But I still thought he was going to fight. I asked him before the induced coma whether he wanted me to send for a priest and he shook his head no. It's a hard thing to watch someone you love pass on, knowing that it is for the best. They must; their time is up. But there is only half of you that sees that. The other half feels totally lost. But he was courageous in dealing with the role that was given to him. My honey died honorably.

Without him I was in shock. The silence was there in our home. The life that was always right there alongside me, breathing with me in our home was not there, is not there, and is never coming back. The daily routine was over—the yogurt, the fruit, and the poems—and is replaced with a nothingness. The feeling takes hold of you in a way that nobody can rehearse for. No one can truly say, "I know what you're going through," because every person's life is different and unique. There's no preparing. I had, thank God, people who at the time I didn't even realize were doing things on their own, who were taking the phone calls, taking messages, answering the cards. I didn't know how to set up the funeral. I certainly wasn't preparing for his imminent death because as far as I was concerned, he was coming back from the hospital.

You should have seen me at the funeral three days after his death. I was the only one not crying. Everybody else was crying hard, and I was the one comforting them. They needed me to comfort them. It was exhausting. There were five hundred people in this little place with everybody weeping and sobbing. It helped me to console them with, "Honey, he's here, he's here, he's not going anywhere." I had to be strong for everybody else, just I like I had to be strong for Jerry when he was in the hospital. I never went to the hospital without makeup on. He knew that every day I put makeup on and I was going to do everything exactly the same way as always. I made sure I put good clothes on because that helped him. Every time I came to the door of his floor I literally did what Roy Scheider's character did in *All That Jazz*. I'd pull myself up, gather my emotions together and think, "It's show time!" I always came in with a smile and a "Hey, honey, how you feeling today?" I didn't want him worrying about me worrying about his dying. And that's the same thing he was doing to me. He didn't tell me bad things because he didn't want to upset me. But going home from the hospital, sitting in a taxi on a dark winter night . . . it was awful. It was 11:30 and he said to me, "Get some sleep." As I shut the door, I emotionally collapsed.

After Jerry passed I never cried in front of people. A lot of people told me that I handled it too strongly. They didn't know that if I had let go I'd have been in tears constantly that first year. I had tissues under every pillow in the house. I cried constantly but not in front of anybody else. It was my loss. I also wouldn't cry in front of them because in talking about Jer, they'd start crying, and now it was my job to say to them that everything is all right. I did that so often. Everybody cried about Jerry, everybody was touched. They thought I was strong because I'd say, "It's all right, he's here." And if I said that they cried even more.

It's so hard to find the words that really express him. Once, I had given him a lapel pin of a little angel with his birthstone on it. He was in the hospital over Christmas and we had decided that we wouldn't give each other presents. On Christmas Day he was still with us and wasn't doped up. He called me over to his bed and gave me a little box. He said, "I wanted to give this to you. Don't be mad." He had sent one of his sons out to get me an angel. Even two days before he passed away, he was thinking of me.

Jerry also wrote the occasional note to me. This one is especially bittersweet.

> *Hi Honey!*
>
> *No Poem, No Joke*
> *I* hate *leaving you for a* day! *But we're going to be rich enough soon so that we can make our own schedule* all year long! *I want to be able to take you any place in the world at any time of the year, and I know that little by little we're getting there!*
> *I love you!*
>
> *XXXX's*
> *Jer*

Jerry always worked at keeping his thoughts positive. He had to fight the fear and doubts but, like in other facets of his life, he learned that a positive attitude was best.

➤➤   ◄◄

Along with fame and riches,
life hands us little glitches.
But I love you
and we'll pull through,
and beat those sons of bitches!

XXXX's
Jer

➤➤   ◄◄

Good morning my love
I hope you are peacefully resting.
I'm off like a loon
but I'll be back soon
when I am all finished with testing!

XXXXXX's
Jer

When Jerry was taking his hormone treatments he had various side effects.

⤜⤚ ⤙⤛

SEPTEMBER 1997

My poor honey bunny
with tummy upset,
and me with the night sweats and such,
if anyone asks if we're sleeping together
you just tell them,
"Not very much!"

XXX's
Jer

Jerry and I thought that laughter gets you through it. He shouldn't have lived for five years after being diagnosed but he kept his immune system strong by taking vitamins and an herbal liquid. It's that liquid that he refers to in the poem as "greeny-water."

JANUARY 2003

You've measured out the coffee,
you've filled the vitamins.
you've mixed the greeny-water
(I'll soon be growing fins).
You've done so many things for me,
how sweet my day begins!

XXXXXX's
Jer

→→   ←←

I've been combing and brushing
and splashing and shaving,
I came up with a thought
that I think is worth saving.
It don't matter how hard
we all try to be wealthy
the main thing we all have to do
is stay healthy!

XXX's (I know, it ain't funny)
Jer

And here is Jerry's poem for his doctor, Richard Bachrach:

To Richard,

You helped my mom to walk again,
kept Elaine away from the "knife."
And then, beyond the call of friend,
you simply saved my life!

Thank You,
Jerry O.

Life Without Jerry

→→　←←

*T*HIS IS MY TEST: how to live the rest of my life without Jerry.

Though he's not with me physically, I am not without him emotionally. Everywhere I go, every walk I take alone, I can see him with me still protecting me, still supporting me. We don't live each of our days as well as we should. You don't appreciate that you feel healthy, or the air is nice, or your hair came out well, or you feel good getting dressed up.

Or that you have someone who loves you.

We do not know what's ahead of us. I always keep telling people, "Always say 'I love you' to those you love, because you never know that you're going to make it back home." A pretty day or a bad day, at least I'm here to see it.

Jerry was an only child, so he always had to entertain himself. He always said that "You can be alone but there's no reason to be lonely. You get a book, there's somebody in that book that you can be with. You can go out and see people. You make yourself lonely." I have to keep this in mind now that I am alone. My life has changed. I didn't know who I was for the first year after Jerry died. Being invited to someone's house for dinner, paying the bills, or hailing a cab, I never did those things by myself. When I walk home at night, my hand wants to reach out and take his, but he's not there.

But you do go on because you have to. I can hear him saying to me, "Get on with your life. I'm still with you. I'm not here but I'm still with you." I don't think a day goes by that I don't hear his voice, see him in the pictures that are all over my home, talk to him constantly, and more often than not, see him in my dreams. Time has a way of easing our sadness and loss, and I appreciate that I was blessed with one perfect man for me. We found each other at the right time, and it blossomed. It was meant to be.

Sometimes the images of Jerry in the hospital, going through those horrible, painful things they were doing for him, come to mind. Those are the images that you try your best not to see in your mind's eye. It's only natural to think of those moments because that was the last time you saw your loved one. Sure, you had years of everyday wonderful things, but that's the last image and that's a terrible thing. You have to go into the healthier times and then the happy times.

I erase those memories with thoughts of the good times, the ordinary day-to-day life we led. Sure, the cruises and the parties we attended were exciting and fun, but I think the true joys in my life were making his dinner, getting the phone call that told me he was on the last scene and would be home soon, cuddling on the couch watching television, me driving a golf cart chauffeuring him around the golf course, and feeling him slipping into our bed when he came home at 2 a.m. fresh from the Lone Star Boat Club after he earned our "unemployment money." Waking in the morning to find two bananas and a poem.

These poems are a celebration of the life until the end . . . until the very end. He really only suffered in the last three weeks of his life when his illness really devoured him. Up to then he always said, "I'm gonna come home."

Our life was easy, our life was loving, our life was filled with laughter. I think about Jerry and me alone in the elevator of our building. He was always tap dancing when we'd ride down in the elevator. He'd quote the comedian Robert Klein and say, "I've got my happy feet, I just can't stop my legs." He would do this crazy, manic tap dance, and we'd laugh and laugh and look like fools when we exited the elevator.

I received hundreds of poems from Jerry, all of which I kept and treasured. Those poems gave me strength and comfort and lots of laughs, but I never wrote my honey a poem. Although I'm not as good with words as Jerry was, here's my poem for him. For the best thing that ever happened to me, the person who gave me love and accepted my love.

For my husband and best friend, this is my poem for Jerry.

Roses are red, violets are blue
my life revolved around loving you.
My heart is filled with memories galore
we had it all and so much more.
So, sleep my "Prince" until it's time
for Heathcliff to find Cathy, his valentine.

XXXXXX,
Elaine

My Wish for You

NOW THAT JERRY IS gone, these poems—hundreds of daily missives, most just jotted on the back of a page-a-day calendar—are among my most precious possessions. Every time I read them, our love feels as fresh and new as it was the first day we fell in love. But in this age of e-mail, text messaging, Twittering, and who knows what else, the old-fashioned love letter is falling out of style. I want to bring it back in vogue.

A love letter doesn't have to be anything fancy—Jerry proved that. Sometimes his poems to me were downright silly! But they were heartfelt, and honest, and I treasure every one more than any of the jewelry or presents he ever gave me. Those notes mean everything to me.

If you love someone, put pen to paper and tell them. You can compose a sweet little rhyme, as Jerry was fond of doing. Or you can just write a regular old letter. Even a simple line or two will do. You don't need fancy stationery (Jerry certainly didn't use any!) or a fountain pen. Your heartfelt words on paper will mean more to your loved one than you can possibly imagine. Here's an idea: start with this . . .

"Remember how I love you . . ."

—*Elaine Orbach, February 2009*

Afterword

by RICHARD BELZER

ELAINE-AND-JERRY, Jerry-and-Elaine: it became one word!

Those of us who knew Jerry and Elaine were so fortunate to experience the love that emanated from them. Working with and becoming a friend to Jerry was a highlight of my professional and personal life. He was a joy to work with: unselfish, professional, and a wonder to behold. He loved to laugh and make me laugh. . . . I was so proud and touched that it brought him such pleasure. His take on the business, his compelling stories, the depth and breadth of his many accomplishments were all a part of this wondrous man.

And then there was Elaine! A darling little force of nature with a sweet and saucy demeanor who adored and perfectly meshed with Jerry in a romance for the ages: the fact that Jerry wrote poems virtually every day for Elaine informs their love with a timelessness that we can all now share in part through this book.

If there is a heaven, then Jerry and Elaine willed it into existence and are there now, together.

—Richard Belzer, 2009

A Letter from the Editor

➤➤   ◄◄

THE AMAZING LOVE STORY of Jerry and Elaine Orbach has a sad coda: just after delivering the final manuscript for this book to her publisher—a book that meant the world to her—Elaine suddenly and unexpectedly passed away in April 2009 of pneumonia. But while she wasn't here to see the finished book come off the press, she knew that by documenting their story, the love she shared with her beloved "Jer" would live on.

Acknowledgments

ANY PEOPLE HELPED AND supported me in the completion of this book. My collaborator, Ken Bloom, is the most important. He approached me the day after Jerry's memorial service and suggested that Jerry's poems and the story of our life together would be worth sharing. Even as a few years passed, Ken steadfastly persisted with the idea. Laura Ross, a former editor of Ken's, also believed in the project and introduced me to Stonesong Press. Stonesong's Alison Fargis became my agent and led me to editor Michelle Howry at Simon & Schuster's Touchstone imprint. Robert Malcolm, Jerry's agent, and now mine, was his usual hilarious and supportive self. Ken's lawyer, Ron Feiner, also helped make this book a reality. Howard and Ron Mandelbaum and the staff of Photofest provided many of the photos in this book. Any success this book achieves is due, in part, to the support of these wonderful friends and collaborators.

Benjamin Bratt, Peter S. Fischer, and Ed Sherin were generous with their memories of working with Jerry. Thanks also to New York City mayor Michael Bloomberg and Dick Wolf for allowing me to quote from their comments made at Jerry's memorial service. All my love to Sam Waterston for his beautifully written and insightful introduction to this book. These coworkers of Jerry's—and, I'm pleased to say, true friends to both of us—have made this a far richer book than it would have been without their contributions.

My dear friends have also been supportive of me during our marriage, Jerry's illness, and my life without Jerry. I'd especially like to thank Jeff Berger, Prof. Richard and Zora Brown, Len and Heather Cariou, Andrea Cohen, Alice Evans, Anita Gillette, Ellen Gould, Rita Hubbard, Susan Johann, Mark Millican, Robin Rose, Catherine Russell, Cheryl Stern, and Linda Gabler Turcell. In addition to many of the above friends, several of Ken's friends read our drafts and gave valuable input. These include Karen Colizzi Noonan, Patricia Plowman, and Josh Wellman. Barry Kleinbort gave me guidance and confidence when I undertook to write my poem to Jerry.

And finally, all my love forever to my dear husband and partner Jerry for giving me a purpose to my life and all the love that can be shared between two people.

About the Authors

JERRY ORBACH was born in the Bronx, New York. He studied drama at the University of Illinois and Northwestern University and then went to New York, where he studied with Lee Strasberg at the Actors Studio.

In his first week in New York, he won the lead role in the historic revival of *The Threepenny Opera*, which starred Lotte Lenya. He next starred in what would become the longest-running show in American theater history, *The Fantasticks*. In that show, Jerry introduced the song, "Try to Remember." He also starred in *Carnival!*, a revival of *Guys and Dolls* (which won him his first Tony Award nomination), *Promises, Promises* (for which he won the Tony), the original production of *Chicago* (another Tony nomination and the best award of all, meeting his wife-to-be, Elaine Cancilla), and *42nd Street*. Jerry Orbach appeared on Broadway more than any other actor in Broadway history.

Following the close of *42nd Street*, Jerry turned his attention to film work in such prominent roles as Jennifer Grey's father in *Dirty Dancing*, a killer in Woody Allen's *Crimes and Misdemeanors*, a tough New York cop in *Prince of the City*, and the voice of Lumiere in Disney's *Beauty and the Beast*.

On television, he starred in his own series, *The Law and Harry McGraw*, which led to the role of Lennie Briscoe in *Law & Order*. Jerry joined the series for the second season in 1992 and stayed with it until 2004. In 2002, he and fellow actor Sam Waterston were named "Living Landmarks" by the New York Landmarks. Jerry quipped to Waterston that they could never be torn down.

Jerry Orbach passed away in 2004 after a long fight with prostate cancer.

→≻   ≺←

Born ELAINE CANCILLA and raised in Pittsfield, Massachusetts, she went straight to New York City at age eighteen. She was awarded a scholarship to George Balanchine's School of the American Ballet. After a year of intense training, Elaine changed venues. Instead of becoming "third swan from the right," she was heading straight for Broadway, where a career of over twenty years was to start.

She worked with the finest choreographers of their time, Peter Gennaro (*Fiorello!*), Michael Kidd (*Here's Love*), and Bob Fosse (*How to Succeed in Business Without Really Trying*, *Sweet Charity*, *Chicago*), to name just a few. She went on to become a "big fish" in the smaller pond of the elite summer stock packages, playing such roles as Sally Bowles in *Cabaret*, Molly in *The Unsinkable Molly Brown*, Charity in *Sweet Charity*, and Anita in *West Side Story*.

It was when Bob Fosse asked Elaine to stand by for Chita Rivera as Velma Kelly in the original production of *Chicago* that she met and three years later married Jerry Orbach. Elaine chose to hang up her dancing shoes for the show-stopping role of Mrs. Jerry Orbach.

Elaine passed away unexpectedly in April 2009, just after delivering the final manuscript for *Remember How I Love You*.

Photo Credits